BUSTA RHYME

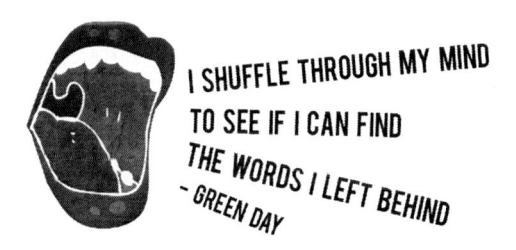

> I SHUFFLE THROUGH MY MIND
> TO SEE IF I CAN FIND
> THE WORDS I LEFT BEHIND
> — GREEN DAY

SOUTH EAST POETS

Edited By Zak Flint

First published in Great Britain in 2017 by:

Young Writers
Est. 1991

Coltsfoot Drive
Peterborough
PE2 9BF
Telephone: 01733 890066
Website: www.youngwriters.co.uk

All Rights Reserved
Book Design by Ashley Janson
© Copyright Contributors 2017
SB ISBN 978-1-78624-892-3
Printed and bound in the UK by BookPrintingUK
Website: www.bookprintinguk.com
YB0303S

FOREWORD

Welcome Reader,

For Young Writers' latest competition, *Busta Rhyme*, we challenged secondary school pupils to take inspiration from the world around them, whether from the news, their own lives or even songs, and write a poem on any subject of their choice. They rose to the challenge magnificently, with young writers up and down the country displaying their poetic flair.

We chose poems for publication based on style, expression, imagination and technical skill. The result is this entertaining collection full of diverse and imaginative poetry which covers a variety of topics - from favourite things and seasons to more serious subjects such as bullying and war. Using poetry as their tool, the young writers have taken this opportunity to express their thoughts and feelings through verse. This anthology is also a delightful keepsake to look back on in years to come.

Here at Young Writers our aim is to encourage creativity in the next generation and to inspire a love of the written word, so it's great to get such an amazing response, with some absolutely fantastic poems. I'd like to congratulate all the young poets in this anthology, I hope this inspires them to continue with their creative writing.

Zak Flint

CONTENTS

Bishop Challoner School, Bromley

Olivia Duggan (11)	1
Millie Barker (11)	2
Mia Emilia Fabrizi (12)	4

Canterbury Steiner School, Canterbury

Jak Taylor (16)	5

Capital City Academy, London

Leigha Sinead Kerr (15)	7

Colchester Institute, Colchester

Tyler-James Collinson (18)	9

Cotelands Pupil Referral Unit, South Croydon

Aaron Bigord (14)	10
Sonny Doke (16)	12
Jessica Storey (15)	13
Louis Brown (14)	14
Rachel Leslie (14)	15
Nour Basyouni (14)	16
Ethan Early (15)	17
Charlie Terence Hierons (15)	18
Claire Ann Greenslade (15)	19

Dover College, Dover

Joseph Christopher Payne-Martinez (14)	20
Angel Golding (15)	22
Vianna Jorgensen (15)	24
Oliver Cheeseman (14)	25
Ryan Sewell (15)	26
Joseph Michael Curran (14)	27
Jack Hanson (14)	28
Angelique Rose Taylor (11)	29
Kirill Babaev (15)	30
Archie Meleady (14)	31
Ben Preusser (14)	32
Isa Mohammed (15)	33
Roosheene Patel (15)	34
Zachary Isaiah Gowon (16)	35
Gabriella Hood	36
Harry Neale (15)	37
Katriona Heritage (16)	38

Dwight School London, London

Gabriel Marc Myers (17)	39
Judy Benichou (16)	40

Gable Hall School, Stanford-Le-Hope

Gracie Nicholls (12)	42
Travis Cox (12)	44
Kibria Akbar (12)	46
Carly Wright (12)	47
Lena Jarvis (11)	48
Femi Olajugbagbe (13)	49
Jude Jolliffe (12)	50
Lily Caddell (13)	51

Eleanor Ling (13)	52
Sophie Rose Runcorn (12)	53

Gregg School, Southampton

Eleanor Wright (12)	54
Georgie Simpson-Silo (12)	55
Georgia Brenchley (12)	56
Freddie Beaver (13)	57
Ricky Chen (12)	58

Langdon Academy, London

Mya Miller-Thomas (12)	59
Ritika Lal Vanyia (12)	60
Druti Ankon Rahman (13)	62
Mubashir Ahmed (12)	63
Roland Warmond Bejenaru (12)	64
Elisa Cosma (12)	65
Jason Adigun (12)	66
Simrandeep Panesar (12)	67
Jessica Kyei (12)	68
Patheswaran Ketheswaran (13)	69
Zohora Ahmed (12)	70
Julius Sabo (13)	71
Hassan Ahmed	72
Yazid Kalil (12)	73
Tashya Kimacia (12)	74
Yolanda Tavares-C (12)	75
Behrouz Garboni (13)	76
Yousuf Hussain (13)	77

Morpeth School, London

Samiul Islam Haider (13)	78
Riyadh Islam (12)	80
Lily Durand (13)	82
Afrida Renu (12)	84
Moyrom Rujena (12)	86
Zaiyyan Salim (13)	88
Shabiha Saleh (13)	89
Serina Chowdhury (12)	90
Rayhan Mahbub (12)	91
Sara Hassan (13)	92

Hamzah Ahmed (12)	93

Palmer's Sixth Form College, Grays

Aron Charles (16)	94
Heather Cutting (18)	98
Lee Thair-White (17)	100

Palmers Green High School, London

Zara Yurtseven (12)	101
Tolani Aradeon (12)	103

Queensmead School, London

Madison Allen (12)	106
Noor Shah (11)	108
Eiman Ali (12)	109
Hewa Hassan (11)	110
Peter Connell (11)	112
Leina Marhoum (11)	113
Francesca Tully (11)	114
Randeep Bhachu (12)	115
Swika Srikanth (11)	116
Aïsha Mancero (11)	117

St Bernard's High School, Westcliff-On-Sea

Isabella Soremi (11)	118

St John The Baptist School, Woking

Emma Alston (12)	120
Georgia Evans (12)	122
Charlotte Saul (12)	124
Shona Ndoro (12)	125

St Mary's College, Southampton

Joshua Abernethy (11)	126
Mia Manreet Kaur Rai (11)	128

Eleanor Smith (11)	129
Inas Kassim (11)	130
Will King (11)	131

Steyning Grammar School, Steyning

Maddi Davis (12)	132
Zoe Ainsworth (11)	134
Cameron Stevens (12)	135
Thea Hayes (12)	136
Oscar Loveridge (12)	138
Alfie Baxter (12)	139
Daniel McGuire (12)	140
Jade Hodges (11)	141
Sophie Martin (12)	142
Katie Ward (13)	143

The Folkestone School For Girls, Folkestone

Fay Burbery (11)	144
Erin Gregory (11)	146
Aimee McCarthy (12)	148
Charlotte Hastie (13)	150
Katelyn Mae Rawlings (12)	152
Zoe Emma Hillman (12)	153
Molly Harding (11)	154
Emma Lowther (12)	156
Chlóe Wallace (12)	158
Lydia Stanton (12)	160
Niamh Emily Simmons (12)	161
Eksha Chongbang (12)	162
Chloe Wiggins (12)	163
Sienna Lukey (12)	164
Harriett Fleur Harper (12)	165
Emily Rose Harlow (11)	166
Lillian Watts (12)	167
Ella Louise Russell (12)	168
Macey Forster (13)	169
Sophie Ida Shield (12)	170
Isobella Church (11)	171
Alice Payne (13)	172
Brooke Marshall (12)	173

Isy Mae Harper (12)	174
Hannah Parry (12)	175
Freya Bailey (11)	176
Olivia Woodland-Owen (12)	177
Lily Miller (13)	178
Lily Bryan (11)	179
Ella Carter (11)	180
Ema Calvo (11)	181
Carla Fleetwood (12)	182
Abbie Conyers (12)	183
Phoebe Reynolds (12)	184
Eve Draper Topping (11)	185
Natalie Burton (11)	186
Georgia Mae Ashman (11)	187

Walthamstow School For Girls, London

Hafsa Moolla (15)	188
Ayan Osman (15)	192
Lily Bea Deason (15)	194
Renette Bakemhe-Moulton (15)	196
Ronja Blight (14)	198
Shahina Jauny (15)	201
Sara Arshad Mehmood (13)	202
Maarya Zahid (14)	204
Aisha Patel (14)	206
Zanib Asim (13)	207
Monika Martinonyte (11)	208
Aliyah Elizabeth Ahmed (15)	210
Zia Ralston (12)	212
Destiny Angela Evelyn O'Kane (12)	214
Imaan Iqbal (15)	215
Ying Hang Zeng (12)	216
Sumbal Arshad (14)	217
Zara Khan (13)	218
Erin Ridgway (12)	220
Samar Mahmood (15)	221
Kiran Tanveer (12)	222
Faiza Mehmood (12)	223
Hannah Billington (12)	224
Emine Ulucay (12)	226
Hannah Rashid (14)	227

Amud Ahmed (12) 228
Samuela Blumel (13) 229
Sergina Sergio (14) 230

THE POEMS

Think Happy

Happiness comes now and then
But no one really knows when
Happiness brings joy and laughter,
And leads to a happily ever after
Happiness will grow and grow
But only if you promise to never let go
Think about what happiness is to you
Is it dancing, singing or the doorbell ringing?
Is it watching TV, debating or roller skating?
Whatever makes you happy, you will notice
A smile on your face that you should embrace
Happiness will grow and grow
But only if you promise to never let go
Never turn off the light to happiness
As happiness is the light in...
You!

Olivia Duggan (11)
Bishop Challoner School, Bromley

I Can See A Rainbow

Green is the symbol of starting over
Green is the colour of a four-leaf clover
Green is a present wrapped in an emerald bow
Or the smallest shoot of spring poking through snow

Blue is the colour of a warm summer sea
Blue is for bright eyes on you and on me
Blue is for wellies that splash on the street
Or a Cookie Monster who likes only to eat

Pink is the colour of hard boiled candy
Pink is the colour of beaches that are warm and sandy
Pink is the colour of a dormouse's tail
Or a boat on horizon with a musky pink sail

Red is the colour of a long-stemmed rose
Red is for Snow White's apple, I suppose
Red is for a blood-red moon up above
Or a beating heart that sends messages of love

White is the colour of a dandelion wish
White is for teeth that end up in a kiss
White is a tissue that covers a sneeze
Or the ghost of a cloud sailing past on a breeze

Yellow is the colour of a warm golden sun
Yellow is for syrup on pancakes by Mum
Yellow puts a smile on everyone's face
Or the colour of daffodils all over the place

Purple is for bunches of violets that please
Purple is for bruises when we fall on our knees
Purple is the colour of queen and her king
Or a song about rain that Prince used to sing

But the colours that describe the world best as you'll see
Are a rainbow, a melting pot, for you and me
We are red, we are yellow, we are colours of each hue
There's a rainbow in us all, I promise that's true

Millie Barker (11)
Bishop Challoner School, Bromley

Think...

Would you think it wise
To be judged by the colour of your eyes?
It's just how you were born
Why would you decide
To make a decision to wreck someone's pride?
It's just what you've been taught
Why would it be fair
To be judged on what you wear?
Does it really matter?
Parents, teachers, children too
Think about if it were you
Think.

Mia Emilia Fabrizi (12)
Bishop Challoner School, Bromley

Is There Hope?

Scraping away at the earth
Ever since their birth
They consume
Slowly sealing their doom
At the earth they grind
And to its damage they are blind

We are nearing the ending
And people still aren't listening
They turn a blind eye
And they don't cry
Humanity's fragrance
Thinking everything's insignificant

They're captives to greed
Hungry to fulfil their need
Desperate to have it all
And through Hell's halls they crawl
Unswayed and unmoved
By what it is that we do

We hang on tight to the rope
Because there is still hope
We still have a chance
There is no such thing as can't
So let's make a difference
And stop this planet from suffering

Let the gunfire cease And let there be peace
Let's bring about change
And love exchange
From this state of violence we must awaken
And stand for peace, unshaken.

Jak Taylor (16)
Canterbury Steiner School, Canterbury

No Pressure

The surrounding area to my eye was grey
All the stress had no measure
This repeated day after day
But hey... no pressure

In order to fit into society
There are certain things you must treasure
To gain them you must lose your sincerity
But hey... no pressure

This journey can be considered slippy
From it you can't gain pleasure
Although to give up would be quite a pity
But hey... no pressure

All these years we've been trained like lab rats
Only made to memorise useless facts
Only to prepare for our SATs and GCSEs
All to put our conformed minds at ease

They give you words to aspire to -
Amazing, outstanding, genius - they only apply to a few
Standardised testing can only make you
Okay, average and normal - the standard student

We're graded on our willingness to obey
So the system spits out words like stupid
But only to those who disobey
Leaving them to become muted

If I'm honest, I'm really quite tired
Most of the day I feel I'm a fool
We're meant to be inspired
Was this really the intention of school?

Mountains of work bestowed upon on
Making my mind a broken tool
Must most teachers do this slaughter spree
Maybe this will be all I gain from school

So in conclusion to my point
Not all qualifications can prevent one from appearing a fool
So they have the power to disappoint
If it's not right for you don't stay in school

But if for you, school is right
It will mean you have no time for leisure
And to stay up to revise all night
But hey... no pressure

Leigha Sinead Kerr (15)
Capital City Academy, London

Time For Tea

Tick-tock goes the clock
As the white rabbit bounds away
Down a hole, far away
Never be late for tea
Wonderland is waiting for you
Tick-tock, tick-tock
You shouldn't keep the Hatter waiting
He is expecting you
Big or small, eat me, drink me
Anything is possible in Wonderland
Is this a dream or is this real
All I know is that you and I
Will meet again soon
On time for tea

Tyler-James Collinson (18)
Colchester Institute, Colchester

Txt Me Pls

'Hi,' pops up on my screen
'Wuu2?' I say rather keen
'Nm,' they reply
'How r u?' I say, feeling like I'm about to die
'Gd, u?' they say
I want to shout, 'No, get out of my way.'
But instead I say, 'I'm OK.'
'U sure?' They're trying to be kind
'Yep,' I say, instead of saying, 'kiss my behind!'

'Wuu2?' It's my turn to be questioned.
'Talking 2 U, lol,' being careful not to reveal my imperfection
'Aha,' they say
It feels like they should've said, 'Go away!'

'You have 17 message requests' pops up on my feed
Only one of them is the person I really need
'I'm bored,' most of them say
'Well, I'm not here to fill your day.'
Sometimes people ask if I'm really okay
It's only because they've had a rubbish day
And they need someone to rant to

'What's wrong?' I say rather subdued
'Nothing, y r u asking?'
'Just wondering, sorry,' I say, trying to avoid a blasting
'Aha,' they say, they don't care for my time, it seems
And they'd much rather look at irrelevant frog memes

That's the problem we have with all the social media
We're expected to be walking, talking encyclopaedias

Aaron Bigord (14)
Cotelands Pupil Referral Unit, South Croydon

Untitled

Innocent at birth
You grow, forced to school
Start thinking it's the worst

Primary school's all fun and games
You don't even remember the names
You're just a child, calm and tame

Secondary school's a lot tougher
Sometimes you want to cry to your mother
And other times you think, *why bother?*

But, it's all worth it in the end
Get your GCSEs and go brag to your friends
And now you can start making amends

Follow your passion
Whether it's dance, music or fashion
If people don't believe in you, then smash 'em

It doesn't matter who you are or what you've done
You can still live a stress-free life that's fun

So carry on, see it through
Don't try to be someone new
Keep it real, and just be you

Now go get what you deserve
And stop being a reserve
Don't think of being second in the race
Because, my brother, number one is your place

Sonny Doke (16)
Cotelands Pupil Referral Unit, South Croydon

Escape

One day sent away
Never allowed out to play
Only nine years old
And already I've been sold

It's a privilege they said
But inside I'm filled with dread
'Don't worry, he will look after you.'
But they will never have a clue

Nine years old and married
Already I've miscarried
I'm expected to have a baby
But all I want is someone to save me

Four years go by
I'm 13 and never been so shy
What if I say the wrong thing?
The threat of removing my ring

I have a baby boy
He has not a single toy
I try to show him what's right
Pray he never tries to fight

My life is forever controlled
Anything good just over the threshold
I wish I could escape
Never to have let them make this mistake.

Jessica Storey (15)
Cotelands Pupil Referral Unit, South Croydon

The Drug

The music is insane
Certain beats activate an electrical wave
Like a burst of electricity directly to your brain
Makes you want to write and continue on with your day
Music is like a drug
It's addictive but motivational
Constantly want to listen to what is being played
Over and over again
We listen to the same songs over and over again
We get the same vibes each time
Till we play it too many times
And when we do that
We find a new song to play over and over again
It's because it's addictive, but it's a good type of addiction

Louis Brown (14)
Cotelands Pupil Referral Unit, South Croydon

Strength

The music I hear is my life
The music I hear is loud
The music I hear makes me feel like
I am floating on a cloud
The music I hear is quiet
As soft as it can be
The music I hear means everything
The music I hear is my key
The music I hear gives me strength
To pick me up every day
The music I hear can always
Help me on my way
The music I hear is a journey
I learn from it every time
Completing itself with a single rhyme
Music is who I am
Music is who I strive to be
Music is all I need
Music will always be me

Rachel Leslie (14)
Cotelands Pupil Referral Unit, South Croydon

The Beauty Is Inside You!

Don't ever give up on what's in your heart
Don't ever let go of what you believe in
Don't ever say that the road is too tough
And that it's better to quit!
Don't ever think that you don't matter
Don't ever think that the world
Doesn't need someone like you
There's magic in you
The beauty is inside you!
That no other could possess a quality, warmth,
A sparkle that will carry you through life's test
Just always remember the beauty is inside you, not them

Nour Basyouni (14)
Cotelands Pupil Referral Unit, South Croydon

You Help Me

In the storm and the rain
God helps us through the game
Even though we are to blame
Jesus died to take the pain

You, God, are my rock
My castle and my shield
For whatever life may yield

God is the potter, we are the clay
You are the reason we live today
Always here when we fear, you keep me near
You are closer than a mother and protect me like a brother

You are my God.

Ethan Early (15)
Cotelands Pupil Referral Unit, South Croydon

Older

I cannot see
I cannot chew
Oh my God, what will I do?
My memory shrinks
My hearing stinks
No sense of smell
I look like hell
My mood is bad!
Can you tell?
My body's drooping
I have trouble cooking
The lonely years have come at last
The lonely years can go straight past

Charlie Terence Hierons (15)
Cotelands Pupil Referral Unit, South Croydon

I Am Happy

I am confident! But I do still have my moments
What really matters is what we feel in our hearts as well
I'm happy, I am me, I am loving, caring
I don't try to be someone I am not
Life is too short to be someone else

Claire Ann Greenslade (15)
Cotelands Pupil Referral Unit, South Croydon

Me

Me
I'm not fixed, I'm not finished
And I'm not ending it here yet

But I'm sick of saying that I feel
No change, I'm tired
Of looking at the same picture
Every day

I'm still unsure of my emotional state
I don't know where I am
I don't know who I am
I miss who I was

I'm always looking up on Google
Trying to find better emotion
Which made me think more
And more how pathetic I was

I can't make decisions
I can't keep promises
I won't be my own friend
And I'm never consistent
I'm distracting myself by playing on the computer
Waiting to get better
When I already know that it won't change a thing

I'm lucky to know greater people
Than most do, but I wish I had
More friends
That I could stand right next to

But when I have the chance to...
I fear being rude or annoying
Being nice but boring, being stupid
And ruthless, being a waste of space
And a waste of time but more
Importantly... useless...

I can't guess what I'll do, I can't ever
Be sure, I am terrified of being
A stupid sheep anymore
I can't face my faults
I can't face my work
But I genuinely believe I am
Capable of changing the world
I still think I can get better
I still think I can find or create
The best version of...
Me.

Joseph Christopher Payne-Martinez (14)
Dover College, Dover

Family

The word 'mum' is one of the most special words
The most comforting I have ever heard
My love for you
Is above all the rest
Mother can I tell you
You are simply the best

Dad you are a hero to me
You're one in a million can't you see?
Each day and night our bond does grow
The never-ending love will forever flow

Since I was a little child
It was clear for me to see
I have such a special family
Who is always there for me!

My sisters, my friends
And all of the above
Not a day goes by when I cannot find this unconditional love!

For my big brother
My little eyes were always watching
Whatever you used to say or do
And when I grew up
Big and tall
I wanted to be just like you
An inspiration and role model
Just for me to see
Imagine if you weren't here, how naughty I would be

Family is one thing everyone will get
Leave them behind and you will only feel regret
Family is one thing that means more than all the rest
Gold, wealth and fortune
No thanks
My family is simply the best

Angel Golding (15)
Dover College, Dover

An Everyday Feeling Of Trepidation

Anxiety crawling all over you
Every single sweat drop gradually reaching your pale cheeks
Only to be swept away
Caterpillars on your skin, transforming into new-born butterflies
Each releasing an intense feeling of doom inside your queasy stomach
Fretfulness is a clock that never stops ticking, a breath that is never released, but only to suffer inside
Making the biggest effort you can to serene your quivering body
But it's never enough to quell the never-ending hurricane
Fear, tension, agitation, doubt, all crammed into an innocent human
Gruelling to survive this trek of experiences
The on-edge suspense chews you up and spits you out
Yet you have never been free of this daunting, cage-like domain
With your head hung low and not knowing where to go
You try to explain but it's all just a mysterious pain
Wherever you go or wherever you are
Influencing your thoughts just to make you over-think everything over and over again
You being to think to yourself
How is this reality?
When is it going to cease?
Little did you know this is just the gun to start to race.

Vianna Jorgensen (15)
Dover College, Dover

Everything Happens For A Reason

As I see my mum get hit and hit
It pushes me till I can't take it
My step-dad tells me I won't make it
Like my emotions I can't fake it
So I spent more time out with my friends
So I can provide more money for my ends
Since I was sixteen I was saving for a Benz
Trying to keep up with the latest trends

I was on the corner sellin' crack
So I can take the debts off my mum's back
I never really had any money
And more and more people started to think it was funny
Every time I think of the estate where I'm from
It reminds me of growing up in London
Going to the chip shop every day
And skipping school on a Friday

So I'm trying to deliver this message to you
No matter where you come from
No matter what you do
No matter how you think
No matter where you move
Everything happens for a reason

Oliver Cheeseman (14)
Dover College, Dover

Bullying

I've experienced the hate through my school year
Taking the mick out of my lifestyle
Pushing me away when I was there
Wouldn't let me talk when I needed help
I thought they were my friends but turned out to become fake friends
They talked about me when my back was turned
They went stabbing me in the back and making it hurt
The one thing I wanted was someone to be there for me
It turned out to be a bad time in my life
When they made fun out of me, my family, my home
It turned into bloody violence
I was going home with cuts and bruises
My mum was asking, 'What's going on?'
I just lied and said, 'It's nothing.'
I was just too scared to say anything in case
They hurt me more

Ryan Sewell (15)
Dover College, Dover

Friends To Enemies

Stabbed in the back by my friend
That brings friendship to an end
Thought we were close, thought we were tight
Had a problem I'd go to you for advice
Don't trust anyone, not even myself
Problems stacking up like a shelf
Don't know what to do anymore
Seems like things don't go right anymore
It's like I'm never happy anymore
Want things back how they used to be
Don't want this pain anymore
Hurt me a lot but can't lie
You're missed
Still hate you though
Wanna give you my right fist
But what's done is done
For us, no going back
Because you stabbed me in the back.

Joseph Michael Curran (14)
Dover College, Dover

The Way You Act

What do you mean, what do you mean?
I'm so cocky, I jump around cos I'm naughty
In my jeans, I'm so swifty
I get peers like it's money

You're so jealous, you can't touch me
You run around spreading stuff about me
But you see it won't touch me
Wanna know why all mates love me?
We are family

All for one and one for all
We believe in what's right, you believe in what's wrong
Thinking you're really strong hurting people
What have they done

But at the end of the day
You will always be wrong
Asking for your mates back
They have gone!

Jack Hanson (14)
Dover College, Dover

Why War?

Why does it matter, black or white?
War is never going to change anything
No matter how hard you fight
People are dying, killing, fighting for land
Rights, greed, envy, even for life happiness
Why can't everyone just be friendly

Have you really thought it through once
War is, war is
The world should be full of peace, not hate
Soon it will be too late
You're killing the Earth with your wars
The fuel kills the nature
Closes all doors

Think before you do
Soon you won't be able to
Help the Earth
Stop the wars
And open up all the doors

Angelique Rose Taylor (11)
Dover College, Dover

The Old Ones

In the dark of the night
In the shadow of light
In the depths of the sea
In the cracks between

Lies his city, his lair

Utter your prayers
As He'll soon be upon all
And will feast on us, devouring whole
There are folk who await His return
They wish to see the world burn
And it's not only him
There are beings unseen
They are up in the sky
Beyond our reach, I imply
They are Horsemen of Apocalypse
Can't negotiate with politics
We have served our purpose
Our demise is certain...

Kirill Babaev (15)
Dover College, Dover

Money And Greed

From day one you were like everyone
Asking for benefits and did not want to work
In the morning till late at night
The next day, do it all again
Waste a bit of money on a scratch card
To see that you have won
From that point on things have changed
From working for someone to owning everyone
What you don't see is that you as a person have changed
You may not see it but everyone else does
You got nastier and greedier and you're losing your friends
You think money is the key to everything
Really it unlocks misery and emptiness

Archie Meleady (14)
Dover College, Dover

Bullying

Bullying is like a cat and a mouse, the cat is the bully and the mouse is the victim
Usually the cat chases the mouse, torturing it and tearing it
The cat lets go and grabs the mouse again
Lets go and grabs the mouse again
Lets go and grabs the mouse again, and it will never stop until the mouse is dead
You're getting bullied?
In an instant you won't notice it
Nasty scars will be left deep and bloody, but they will never heal
Guilt and anger will replace your once calm and peaceful life

Ben Preusser (14)
Dover College, Dover

Life Of A Gangsta

Three shots in the dark
I'm like a dog with a bone
You won't see me coming

I'm like a ghost
You won't see me coming
This fire is about to ignite
It's gonna be lit

Let me show the life of a gangsta
It's not about the banter
It's about the *bang! Bang! Boom! Boom!*
You won't see me coming

This life is hell
It's like I'm stuck in a cell
You won't see me coming

Isa Mohammed (15)
Dover College, Dover

Poem Hostage

Roses are red
Violets are sort of blue
I was forced to do this poem
And probably so were you

They made me write
Wouldn't let me leave
This poem is going
To be the end of me

Had to make up rhymes
Without any assistance
Been here four days now
I need persistence

No food, no water
Wrote three stanzas, I'm proud
Decided to call it a day
I'm free now

Roosheene Patel (15)
Dover College, Dover

Wine?

Time and time
Life and dine
Time and wine... question mark

Is that your life?
Giving it away to time
With wine and a little bit of lime

Because death will chase you
In a matter of time

Don't waste your life
Don't die for wine after your life
It will have another
It's not your friend, nor is it mine
My life is mine
I don't need some more wine.

Zachary Isaiah Gowon (16)
Dover College, Dover

Cruelty To Animals

Humans are beasts,
When they strike they're like vultures,
Swooping in to devour the vulnerable mice,
Or hyenas laughing, jeering and taunting
the innocent meerkats that are unsure of their fate,
Why are people so despicable?
There is not an immense difference between us,
Except we're the big, bad, scary wolf,
Animals are Little Red Riding Hood,
Exposed to the world.
Stop this cruelty now!

Gabriella Hood
Dover College, Dover

The Months

January is quite cold
February comes along
March is quite bold
April birds sing their song

May it comes and goes
And then there is June
July comes with no woes
August the flowers have bloomed

September introduces chills
And then there is October
November starts with bills
December, a time to remember

Harry Neale (15)
Dover College, Dover

Four In One

The crunchy, crispy chestnut-coloured leaves falling down from the autumn trees
The sparkling, shimmering snow laying on the ground like a white blanket
The disappearance of spring and the sound of the busy, buzzing bees
The blazing summer sun shining all day until the hour of sunset

Katriona Heritage (16)
Dover College, Dover

Forbidden Fruit

Who would've guessed?
You and I abreast
Not only in friendship
But the love we possess

Our minds coincide
Our 'sins' justified
When we're lip to lip
There's nothing to hide

Standing proud
Where disallowed
We fought with passion
To join the crowd

Our infatuation grew
Trust and faith accrued
Dirty by nature
Or so we were viewed

And there are those who disagree
Society plagued with psychology
Weep and watch us fall to our knees
As Mother Nature injects her disease

Our sacred relation shall never perish
For forbidden fruit is what I cherish

Gabriel Marc Myers (17)
Dwight School London, London

Silence Of The Crows

I am a melting pot of slavery
My ancestors - each a link in the chain
Shackled by the memory of the bitter taste of our pain

Jewish and black, sounds like a joke in a bar
Yet as the master of blue and white stands above
Guns blazing, eyes filled with amazement, as she hits the pavement
Here lies another black sister who won't ever make it

And if I don't make it? I'll be torn down
Cos a black or a Jew can't wear the crown
It's not my honesty that got me the place
So I wait at the kerb, the punchline awaits

Sometimes I close my eyes
Not to see the shine of my difference
I see disgust, deference
And I don't wanna make light of my situation
But this is my place in this nation
Where the shame I feel in my reflection
The daily news reel of imperfection

Sitting silent in a room
My presence, deafening
But the future beckons and a plan that reckons
I look around at a changing world
The power of hate is fading

No long paint strokes of God's hand divide
Our fellow brothers (and sisters) watch each other with pride

Our arms aloft, our hearts abandoned
Choirs singing of freedom and peace
Of a story that dripped
From blood-stained lips of ancestors
To us, finally, children erupted from the children
Who have risen and rise and rise
Against injustice - deprived

So, we live on
Deaf to the Crows of the past
To fulfil the destiny of a King
To enjoy
Speak together in tandem
So long to those on the kerb
Lingering on corners waiting to destroy

Goodbye you madmen.

Judy Benichou (16)
Dwight School London, London

You Know

You know you have the perfect life
Some people are barely escaping the knife
That girl, she lives in Aleppo, lost her father last night
He had no chance, couldn't even put up a fight
Now she's alone
Sad, her father, her hero wasn't even known

That girl, she lives in Kenya, walked miles for contaminated water
She's raped, used for money, how could you let that happen to your daughter?
She's used as a genie, she grants their wishes
She works for food; walks for water, everything to washing the dishes
She doesn't go to school either, but he can?
What, just because he's a man?

You know that boy, he lives in London, his mother hit him last evening
He's got a puce bruise now, what's your excuse, you're still grieving?
He never thought for one minute he'd never see his father again
He misses the laughs, the smiles, oh the pain

You know that new born, he lives in Ethiopia, he's doomed to die from malnutrition
He'll be helpless, weak and put on television for exhibition
But nothing ever changes does it, they're still knocked out like flies
His mother puts on a brave face, but when alone she breaks down and cries

The woman, you know, lives in Rio, her husband left her with two kids and barely any money
He thinks it's a joke, he thinks it's hilarious, trust me she's not finding it funny
They're on the brink of starvation, she works day and night, but it's never enough
It's only a matter of time before they too are sleeping rough

See you, you have the perfect life
Some people are barely escaping the knife
You sit and moan about the dinner, or that you need the new phone
At least you are not wasting away to skin and bone

Gracie Nicholls (12)
Gable Hall School, Stanford-Le-Hope

'Mad Is It Not?'

I am the smoke of the flame
Everyone but not me
I can't think, hear or see
Nor nose or mouth functions
But tongues I have many

Is it not mad?

I am as you are as I am to me
As I am to my world
As your world to you
As we are to this world
As this world to you

It is not mad!

Listen clearly and speak as me;
'I have ears, eyes and a mouth
However, no chin or nose south
Sanity I am short of.'
Be of help to us, friend

Not mad is it?

'Madness!' yells I, 'madness,' I say
This is what keeps me sane
I wish to go back, back to words
Books and letters the same!
None of this is fun
I wish to end your game!

Not mad it is!

We can't have that, can we?'
You're only at the beginning
You are to wander round in squares
Until nothing you understand
Read your wish, bored you mustn't be

It is not mad?

This question you must answer
Little time I will give
Time you had always little
Tongues we have and yet
Sense we make little

Not; mad it is!

We are the smoke of the flame
Everyone but not us
We can't think, hear or see
Nor nose or mouth's function
Tongues... many have we.

Travis Cox (12)
Gable Hall School, Stanford-Le-Hope

Being A Muslim

I am Muslim, I am proud!

All praise is to Allah,
Glory to Him the exalted,
Because of this I am never insulted,
And illness of my heart stays afar.

Islam is peaceful and calm,
It teaches all to be great people,
Holds our happiness at our palm,
It shows right from wrong on an easel.

I am Muslim, I am proud!

The Prophet Muhammad
Peace be upon Him,
He would give life and limb
To get his message heard and read,

Not alone was He,
More messengers like Him were sent,
To spread the word of religion and deen,
And what they had said was meant,

As they were the words of Allah,
All forgiving, all merciful.

I am Muslim, I am proud!

Kibria Akbar (12)
Gable Hall School, Stanford-Le-Hope

She Was Fine

You could see deep down into her soulful eyes
She just wanted to end her tiresome life
Although she seemed so strong
There was something wrong
She was fine

Always she wished
One day she might finally be missed
She could run away in her dreams
Where she wouldn't have to shout or scream
She was fine

It was only a matter of time
Before she really wasn't fine
She was fine
She kept telling herself that
All she needed was someone to have a chat

But she was alone
Forever alone
She would wear her brave face
Hoping no one would see
She did need to be saved
She really did need to be saved

Before
It was too late
She wasn't fine

Carly Wright (12)
Gable Hall School, Stanford-Le-Hope

Save Big Cats Now Or It Will Be Too Late

If I were a big cat
I wouldn't want to become extinct
My friend was killed the other day
He really should have run away
Most big cats run away from poachers within a blink
But no, not this one, he didn't think
So within one shot, he was dead
Within half a day he was never seen again
I wouldn't want to be hunted
So help me and all the other big cats out there
Live our lives and never be scared
Or get captured by the evil poachers who want to make
A few bucks
By ending our lives and stealing our coats
So please save us, as now
You are the only hope
If I were a big cat
I wouldn't want to become extinct

Lena Jarvis (11)
Gable Hall School, Stanford-Le-Hope

Winter

The cold December breeze drifts through the air
It's the time the days are getting shorter
Soft, small snowflakes fall down without a care
Kids, thrilled - Christmas is around the corner
Icicles hang down gently from the roofs
Late night carriage rides in New York City
Imprints in the snow from the horses' hooves
Fairy lights hung - everything is pretty
Shop shelves stocked up with mince pies and puddings
The atmosphere is filled with cosy scents
Hung by the warm fireplace are stockings
All excited for the coming events
This is winter in all of its glory
Now is the end of a year long story

Femi Olajugbagbe (13)
Gable Hall School, Stanford-Le-Hope

Football

Football is chess
One wrong move
And our team is a mess
Players are key
Like teabags in tea
And some cost a very big fee!

The managers decide
Whilst the players ride
Football's like the weather
No matter how good it could always be better
Clubs search for the next big thing
Which will earn them loads of bling bling
Some players have skills
But some are only there for the dollar bills

Football may not be here forever
But it brings so many people together
Whether you like it or not
One thing's for sure
Football will not be forgot

Jude Jolliffe (12)
Gable Hall School, Stanford-Le-Hope

Hand In Hand

Together they walk
Ignoring the chants
Ignoring the talk

They had never felt
Such discrimination
They had no choice
It's part of their creation

'Love is love!' they cried
In their own little bubble
How desperate they were
To burst out of the rubble

They screamed
They bawled
No one heard them
Yet they still crawled

They'd had enough
They did it on their own
They found their strength
They overcame the homophobes

Lily Caddell (13)
Gable Hall School, Stanford-Le-Hope

Summer

O summer joy
People engrossed in seasonal fun
Dancing under the auburn sun
The beautiful sea waving back at me
My face is filled - I smile with glee
Daydreams and ice creams
The crystal sand is warm like the embers of a barbecue
It tickles my skin
Joy

Playing in the park
Out until dark
Swinging high
Almost touching the cheery sky
Admiring the vibrant flowers
Staring at the tall tree towers
Puffy clouds grinning
Little girls singing
Laughter
Happiness
Joy

Eleanor Ling (13)
Gable Hall School, Stanford-Le-Hope

Disappearing

Lost, I'm stuck, falling, falling, gone. Lungs shrivelling,
breath quickening, slowly, slowly, gone. I can hear
their voices, quieter, quieter. Gone. Ears tingling,
feet kicking, crying, crying, gone. I'm a
spinning whirlpool of confusion. My
life's just an illusion. It's coming
to a conclusion. Words printed
inside my head. Feet heavier
than lead. Lifeline slowly
sinking, dead. As fast
as a Cheetah,
life forever
Gone.

Sophie Rose Runcorn (12)
Gable Hall School, Stanford-Le-Hope

Abusing Dogs

Dogs, they are never the same
Some are soft, some are coarse
Some are lazy, some are lively
Some are yappy, some are quiet
Some are speedy, some are slow
Dogs come in many kinds
You have
Cocker Spaniels
Cockapoos
Labradors
So many more
Why do you abuse them? They help the world
We have:
Search and rescue
Police dogs
Fire dogs
Sniffer dogs
So many more
Why abuse them? They help us so much

Eleanor Wright (12)
Gregg School, Southampton

Sold

I was bullied
I was cold
No one liked me
So I was told

People took me
I was left as a slave
I was gone so very far away

My back was burning
It was like fire
The whip was so very like a tyre

I was stuck
I was crying
It was like I was dying

Then that day came
It would have never been the same
Because I was sold

Georgie Simpson-Silo (12)
Gregg School, Southampton

Waiting...

Standing still
Hearts open, waiting for love
I heard voices from above
I still remember the soft cry
I could hear myself waving goodbye
I walked along the cold streets
Never looking back
I heard a song in my head
A song I almost remembered

'Wait here she said,'
She never came back
And here I am walking alone
On a street called Homeless Town

Georgia Brenchley (12)
Gregg School, Southampton

Granny

Granny, what a wonderful woman.
She would look after you when you don't feel the brightest.
She will always be there for your troubles.
If you need picking up from your late night clubs,
she will pick you up.
But then the time has come,
to say goodbye to your loved one,
and it's time to move on.

Freddie Beaver (13)
Gregg School, Southampton

Friends

Friends are always there for you
No matter what the problem is
Friends help you as much as they can just for you
Friends are people who you miss
You miss your friends after a long holiday
And forty-eight-hour weekends
Even during long school days
They will be with you till the end

Ricky Chen (12)
Gregg School, Southampton

Olympic Dream

I'm going to the Olympics
I'm going to win gold
To do so I have to be strong
To do so I have to be bold

I'm representing my country
I'm doing so with pride
My name is Mya Miller-Thomas
And soon my name would be world wide

Standing and waiting for the race to begin
I'm getting quite nervous
Thinking, *am I going to win?*

Crouching down low waiting for the gun
Bang! There it goes
We're starting to run
I'm sprinting as fast as I can, I'm going to burst
Come on legs, keep going, I wanna come first
Just one last metre I cross the line
Am I first? Am I last? And what's my time?
I stand on the podium, proud and bold
I'm wearing my medal, it's a Olympic gold.

Mya Miller-Thomas (12)
Langdon Academy, London

Love!

Love!
What does this word mean to you?
Love! Think!
To me, love is tough
When people call you buff
You think you're all rough
This is what they all think
But is this what you call love?
Relationships!
They all give you tips
But you know they're all fibs
But is this what you call love?
You got love for your father, your mother
Your sisters, your brother
But it's all sort of a cover
Then suddenly you find your lover
And you don't look back ever
But is this what you call life?
Care!
If you care you wouldn't let someone's heart tear
I know love is a bit rare
But everything in life has to be fair
But is this what you call love?
Happiness!
It's all a bit luminous
You want everything to be fabulous

Every moment is precious
But is this what you call love?
And once again, I ask you
Love!
What does this word mean to you?
Love!

Ritika Lal Vanyia (12)
Langdon Academy, London

Perfect

What is being perfect?
Does it mean to be beautiful, cute and attractive?
Or does it mean to be intelligent, kind and supportive
Why do people want to be perfect?
Is there a specific reason behind it?
No one in this world is fully perfect
Each and every one of us has some good qualities
And some bad qualities
Here is a short, sad story
About a girl came Daysy
She was perfect, or she thinks that she is perfect
She was cute, pretty and beautiful
She used to bully everyone
She used to think every one wasn't perfect, only her
No one used to like her
One day she was spying on a popular girl in her school
She saw she was kind, supportive and helpful
She realised that beauty doesn't mean anything
Once, again, no one is perfect! No one!

Druti Ankon Rahman (13)
Langdon Academy, London

Work

Work, work, such an elegant thing
People run to work
While
Working to burn off fat
They choose to walk
It is called work
You are dragged down by work
With no chance of crawling back up again
Books, cooks, looks
All incomplete without work
School, classes and teachers all waiting
To fill your weight with two times your height of work
End of the day
Ah, relaxing time is it... No work
Is always with you
Revising, visiting, searching
For more work
Jobs, universities, companies
All with people carrying work on their tireless backs
Will we ever be alone
And in a world where were things just...
There
And no work
The answer is up to you
And you alone.

Mubashir Ahmed (12)
Langdon Academy, London

Racism

Racism. Everywhere you go. Racism
No matter what time, what place. Racism
From houses to bus stops to schools to hotels
Racism
Bang! Shots fired, racism
Families broken just because of racism
They say you can fix what you started but you can't
Racism
Just because a few idiots like Trump,
The world will never be peaceful
The spark to wars. Racism
We are all equal
'It is not our differences that divide us.
It is our inability to recognise, accept
And celebrate those differences.'
This was said but then *bang!*
To stop racism there is nothing we can now do.

Roland Warmond Bejenaru (12)
Langdon Academy, London

Fear

If I could take your issues
I would toss them all into the sea
But all these situations I'm finding
Are impossible for me
When we close our eyes at night
The war we just began to fight
Visions of light disappear
All the nightmares reappear
Bombs are flying in the air
Gases spreading everywhere
All my screams no one will hear
As I cry and shiver in fear
Why would God allow these things?
War and horrifying things
Soldiers fight like cats and dogs
All that's heard is booms and bombs!
I see my dreams fading away
As my heart breaks day by day

Elisa Cosma (12)
Langdon Academy, London

Disappointing Death

Death is most painful
Death can't be paid for
Which one of us can take death?
We can't because it takes our breath
Well if we stop this
We can help
Poor kids dying
All I can hear is people crying

Flying bombs going over our heads
How many people are dead?
We don't know
Because the world just flows
At the time it flew by
But we don't know how many people died
So that's why I cry
Also I pray to this day
That war will stop
Because it is getting hot
Please stop!
Please stop!

Jason Adigun (12)
Langdon Academy, London

Jealousy

What really is jealousy?
Is it that emotion that makes you feel good inside?
No!
Or is it those tears that never dried?
Jealousy is really a poison of the mind
It always rots your tongue
It feels like getting stung
But remember
Haters only hate things they can't have
Bossing you around like sat-navs
Never hate people who are jealous of you
But instead, respect their jealousy
Because you're a reflection of what they wish to be
Just live your precious life
And your troubles will disappear you'll see

Simrandeep Panesar (12)
Langdon Academy, London

Hate!

We're all the same
But we all got a different name
Why do you think differently?
Some people are lame and some are for the fame
People dying
Children crying, *boom!*
You're on the ground
That one gunshot changes everything
You hear people saying, 'Please come back!'
People can't put a stop to the attack
You lie there cold-blooded, thinking you're coming back
But wait
Wait...
This is how it was all patterned
Why did it all change?

Jessica Kyei (12)
Langdon Academy, London

Terrorism

T hese tragedies are occurring too often in today's society
E veryone is affected, be it directly or indirectly
R easons? Could they tell us any that would forgive their sins
R esentment and remorse they do not feel, these horrible
O rganised and planned attacks on the
R espectable, innocent people who are unknowing
I rreplaceable lives in an instant because of these
S elfish, terrorist acts of
M urder

Patheswaran Ketheswaran (13)
Langdon Academy, London

Poverty

Her mum and dad are crying
She's starving
No home, no food, no happiness in life
She's dying, dying

She's suffering
No survival, no freedom of the pain
It's killed her inside
She's dying, dying

She knows what's coming to her
She knows there is no survival for her
Unless she has hope
But what hope? When...
She's dying, dying.

Zohora Ahmed (12)
Langdon Academy, London

Goal!

Goal!
Sabo the only soul in the team
I'm so mean I go past players in my sleep
Taking a sneak peek at my future trophies
All of a sudden all hear is *beep, beep, beep*
Driving home in my jeep
I'm trying to remember what happened to my knee
It's fractured, my dreams captured
Trying to recover, calling my mother
If only my brother continued
Our dream.

Julius Sabo (13)
Langdon Academy, London

War...

War...
Children cry
Mothers die
Lots of conflicts
People running
Because later
We will have nowhere else to be
Just like that little kid Lee
He just wanted to be free
And he was just three
We could have let him be
He just wanted to look into the future years
And just open your eyes
To a world that can shine
We will be just fine...

Hassan Ahmed
Langdon Academy, London

Refugees!

Those who survived a brutal death
Losing all family and friends to a group of masked men
Vile, brutal and cold-blooded
Those who have survived lay in devastation, isolation
Every single second scared to death, worried about their mischievous future
Walking 15km a day, trying to find a home, *boom!*
In a second, millions of lives washed off the planet...

Yazid Kalil (12)
Langdon Academy, London

We Can't Escape It

Death is ungrateful
Very hateful
Whatever we do
We can't escape it

We try and try
Why don't we just
Give up
It's nearly the
End of time!
We can't escape it

It comes knocking
With no warning
Next time we'll
Be mourning
Death!
We can't escape it

Tashya Kimacia (12)
Langdon Academy, London

Love

People will love you
They will hate you
They'll be so ungrateful
Most people live
They can't forgive
She they'll enjoy the painful
So many lives
They can't survive
But we just keep on going
It's like that time
The bullets fly
And they just kill the vibe!

Yolanda Tavares-C (12)
Langdon Academy, London

The War

Looking around
The battle scene
Was harsh
The bodies were scattered
It was atrocious
The scent of blood was
Surrounding me
Bang! Bang! It still carries on

Behrouz Garboni (13)
Langdon Academy, London

Hate

I'm filled with anger
Had a brother
Had everything
But now
Got a dagger
Lost a brother
I'm filled with fire
Everyone's a liar
Everyone will pay!

Yousuf Hussain (13)
Langdon Academy, London

Corruption

It is everywhere (corruption)
It is a volcano waiting for its eruption
For them it's like a trend
But corruption you cannot mend
They are the trend-setter
Most follow them because they
Said they'd make our world better
They take our taxes and spend
It on war, therefore there
Is some reason that the homeless
Are still living raw day by day
Getting more poor
Where does our money go?
If to other countries we still owe
Why do we pay so much tax
Ammunition and guns, loans
Pay rise spent to the max
These people are society's jewels
So apparently they are the
Only ones allowed to bend rules
They are the most cruel, two-faced and thieving group
Their leadership is one, big, concealed and demonic yearly loop
If you know the truth you better keep quiet
Otherwise 'anonymous' groups will get together and create a substantial riot

We are leading your world into a state of calamity
They can wait and wait for you to break
Break a law so you can go into a state of criminality
They wish to be biased
They don't care
Everyone calls them liars
Still following the system
People try to rise with them
And metaphorically kiss them
Carry on, carry on, go on
They take down each con
No one links back the blame
From where it came
As lame as they are
They do it for fame
Just know we are the corrupted corruption
We wait for our eruption
They have you idle, you do not understand
That we need to make a stand
These people make problems but now they are
Taking control over the world with a coup
But right now they are building it up
By stirring everything like as stew
Some knew
Corruption by the name of:
Government.

Samiul Islam Haider (13)
Morpeth School, London

Football poem

Pass the ball
Pass the ball
Pass it to me
Can't you see that I'm totally free?
Push them
Barge them
Down to the ground
Just don't worry
It won't be a foul
Come on defenders
Be more strong
No, no defenders
You've got it all wrong
Let's go strikers
On the attack
Defenders have tackles
Strikers fall back
Look at the scores
It's two all
Come on
Let's try to boost up the scores
Look at the time
Just one minute
One more attack
We won't be able to do it
Yes striker
You've got the ball
Whoosh, past defenders
Give it your all
You've scored, you've scored

We can't believe it!
The time is up, shouting, 'We did it!'
Look at the manager
Leaping in the air
We run to him
Dancing everywhere
Look at all of us
Standing with the cup!
Waving hands to the fans
Yelling, 'We never give up!'

Riyadh Islam (12)
Morpeth School, London

Kindness

A few months ago, I was hiking in
Snowdonia
A pack on my back
Running
Down
Snowdon
With my friends
Yet we were silent
Thinking
Peaceful
The sun's rays shone down
Onto my aching neck
And I asked myself
What does this feel like?
I wanted everyone in the world to feel what I felt
But what was it?
Peace? Happiness? Love?
Kindness? Kindness?
I've heard stories of loneliness
Grief
Despair
Sadness
I have heard stories that brought tears to my eyes
Shivers to my shoulders
Pain to my heart
Why? Is all I ask
Why do you have to put me down
To bring yourself up?

Why does your happiness depend on my self-esteem weakening?
Because every time you open your mouth to make a joke, it drops
Explain that
Two things make up humanity:
The strive to survive
The need to love and feel loved
Why does the latter rely on others' unhappiness?
Why can we not be at peace with one another?
Why can we not have a little kindness?

Lily Durand (13)
Morpeth School, London

My Fame, My Freedom

My aspirations, my dreams
My motivations, high-hoping pleads.

I am slowly turning into a captivating butterfly,
and soaring through the open sky

Flashing lights, here, there, everywhere,
just giving the world my rightful share

Instagram, Snapchat, Twitter and more
My jaw-dropping, worldwide fame galore

My infinite surroundings, people, shoes, dresses, glitter, pink and statement necklaces
Big ones, small ones, oddly satisfying ones, intricate ones, colourful ones and over-shining ones

What would you choose? Either:
Be locked up in a cage with ferocious tigers biting down on their razor-sharp teeth... or...
Roam the acres of lush meadows while smelling the fragrant, memerising flowers?
I choose the meadow
My freedom represents me, my freedom is my life
Leaving the drain with my worries and my strife

Each step you take
Each move you make
Each promise you break
Each life at stake Each mouth-melting cake Oh for my mother's sake

Each chapter you enter, whether minimal, colossal or out of the ordinary, you've got to know, enjoy your life

Afrida Renu (12)
Morpeth School, London

My Personal Feelings

Things that make me sad in life
Bullying, bullying means a lot in my life
That one word, bullying, makes me feel so sad
Reading, replacing, relaxing makes me feel happiness around
Loving, liking, landscapes reminds me of being on holidays all year round
The past can bring back many old memories
So will the future, so be really excited
Racism makes me angry
I think all humans should be treated equally
No human in this world should be treated unfairly
No more suffering or torture
One day when you will be walking down the street
You will ask yourself, 'Have I ever been bullied?'
You tell me that
The stars shine the brightest
On the darkest nights
But you see
Not everyone is a star
Not everyone is as beautiful
Not everyone can catch your eyes
Nobody in this world is perfect
Don't judge a person on their character
Don't judge a person on their looks
Because everyone is different

But can remain equal
Because this is who I am
This is me

Moyrom Rujena (12)
Morpeth School, London

Colours

There's black and white, brown and pale
Back in the day some were hammerin' a nail
There's no need to be racist we are all equal
We are a giant community full of people

Why be a racist, it's really bad
But if you choose to be one you're really sad
You see a white or pale, they're perfect as a gem
But you see a brown or black, you think they cause mayhem

Any skin colour you call them a name
It's not going to get you any damn fame
All the people that are racist, you are pathetic
To be honest, you should be apologetic

There's black, white, brown and pale
Back in the day some were hammerin' a nail
There's no need to be racist, we are all equal
We are a giant community full of people

Zaiyyan Salim (13)
Morpeth School, London

A Secret No One Knew

I was thrown away into the deepest sea
Never to learn
Never to sleep
My hatred has been placed inside my heart
I shed crimson blood cut by reality
My dreams are shattered
Thoughts in my head endulging me
Knife by my neck
It's killing me
Help me! It's an emergency!
I wanna throw everything away and run
To the deepest forest where no soul can judge
A place where I can hide by myself
That's what I want
But that's a desire that can never come true
It's time I told someone
It's time someone knew
Although the fear and insecurities
Will always live in my head
It's something to learn from
Because no fear
Will be such a fear
If that fear is dead

Shabiha Saleh (13)
Morpeth School, London

Mum

Shall I compare thee to a shooting star
A shooting star that brightens up my life
The amazing, glistening moon you are
You are the brightest star in my life
You light me up inside like the 4th of July
I love to see you shooting across the night
You shine so bright and stand out in the sky
When I look up, I see you shining bright
Your light is a force that can't keep me away
You are the most beautiful star in my life
I stare at you in wonder as I lay
Your amazing points are as sharp as knives
Our love cannot be crushed like an unstable plane
I love you more than words can explain

Serina Chowdhury (12)
Morpeth School, London

Education Is A Situation

Education, education
Education is sometimes fun
But sometimes education is so dumb
Sometimes it can even make you numb
Overwhelming!
Education is amazing
But sometimes it's eyebrow raising
Some think of education as an irritation
But others may think education is a satisfaction
But those who would die for an education
They probably live in a terrible situation
So your situation is like a new kind of haven
So remember those in terrible situations
So don't think of your education as such an irritation

Rayhan Mahbub (12)
Morpeth School, London

Schooling The Haters

You hate me for my colour
You hate me for my skin
You hate me if I'm fat
You hate me if I'm thin

You hate me for being a woman
Or even a gay man
You hate me for my disability
Just cause I can't and you can

But it's your brain that's dark
And it's your heart that's blind
And it's your stubborn character that refuses to open its mind
If only you would listen and see the world anew
You will then realise that your kind are few

Sara Hassan (13)
Morpeth School, London

Home

Sad little goldfish swimming in a tank
Dreaming of a lush green, river bank
Trapped behind the glass, wishing for the sea
Hoping for the day that he could be set free

His lonely little face
Brought sadness all around
Like a child's dream getting stamped on
The heart yearned, to be found

Hamzah Ahmed (12)
Morpeth School, London

Where Are We? What's Going On?

Where am I?
What's going on?
Who am I?
Have I just woken up?
Or have I just gone back under?
No. It feels like a break from sedation
Sedation being the preaching of ignorance
And ideological suppression
Am I thinking in opposite?
Is this the wrong - no it feels liberating
The right way to think
This is strange. What's going on?

I can see more
Something tugging on my arms and legs
The strings are thin and silk, just about visible
A pyramid further in the distance
Everything's now suddenly... miserable:
A shape creeping, corrupting the brightness
The curtain behind the order
The suits pulling the strings
The darkness now at every border
My world is changing. Where am I?

I used to feel so loved and cared for, that was the system
Our wants and needs were taken care of, all we had to do was listen

But now I feel poisoned
My integrity reaching expiration
Was I just part of a simulation?
Am I just a glitch?
A bug?
Either way I'm still on my own
I now realise
To those above: I'm just property
We're just kept in a bubble
Outside's a monstrosity
The first world disguises the inhumanity with false honesty
This is the truth
But I feel to reject it
With this type of knowledge... My mind is infected
And now I'm just a parasite to society
Broken from the general cult of personality
This new intelligence feels like a detriment
Is this control all for our well being?
Or am I just a corrupted being?
Or is this for them?
Is this repression?
My perception of the world has been altered
Acuity of the world about to be restructured. What's going on?

It's come to me, now I realise
With these new real eyes
Life is straight up paradoxical
When we're sedated all we want

Is to know it all
I now see that we made the pyramid...
That we're just tools
The suits at the top keep the IV coursing
Pulling our strings so we can hold their board
We're just puppets playing chess
We play against each other and all they do is rest
Increasing the dosage so we don't get the message
I now sense the world's true essence;
Fuelled by power and corruption
I smell the inevitable destruction
Nothing can be done
This is Hell
I'm trapped in this. Where am I?

See all we have to do is stand up
But their powers paralyse us
Restricts us of reason
Thinking past the system isn't prejudice, it's treason
This is the punishment I get
I'm just here, going through the motions
All I have are these broken socially engineered emotions
I'm overwhelmed, I see past the barrier of illusion
Surrounded by the dark remnants of sedation
There are no credible solutions
Most I can do is inflict fear in the suits
Making the 1% aware of the inevitable danger
But I can't, I'm just a wayfaring stranger
As the others march on, I'm left behind

With this new illusion of awareness invading my mind
This is the paradox, I've been conquered
Hopes and dreams diminished with this path I chose
Questions remain unanswered
The spiral goes deeper and darker
I can't
I want to go back, what's going on?

Aron Charles (16)
Palmer's Sixth Form College, Grays

Youth Regime

14, 12, 10, 8, 6
Numbers to you,
Expectations for us.

Cogs spun round so fast
Youth doesn't seem to last.
Media manipulation of image -
From creases of slick paper

Despite folds being abhorrent
When adorned the body.
Vessels of greed
Buckles down your weight

Society rules, half the age
Rips out the pages of the young,
Facts of the former turn into fiction.
Story-telling no longer.

Statements to be read.
Youth fleeting, ripped apart
Reaching social climbs
As vital as your heart.
Pulled and morphed
Like flowers in a storm
Wind blows change

Ringlets smothered the face
Are now ironed out in its place.
Guided in a queue,
Sectioned row of conventional order

Expectations for us
Implemented by you

Heather Cutting (18)
Palmer's Sixth Form College, Grays

You Don't Have To See To Feel

Even in the dark my skin is crawling
I can't see the curve of my hips
The shape of my lips as the corners tug down
I can't see the way that my eyes glisten
Unshed tears that would blur my vision

I can see my body as if it were glowing
Instead all of my insecurity is showing
When my hand drags across my jaw
And all I feel is smooth, hairless skin
The thing that pushes my knees to the floor

The carpet scrapes and scratches there
Like the words thrown carelessly, unfair
In the way that they just don't care
I see their hate, it festers in the air
Even after their voices fall silent

Sticks and stones, they say to me
But please, surely, you can see
That to me those words cut in deep
To the root of me that will always believe
Freak, tranny, f*****, f**
Is all that I will ever be...

Lee Thair-White (17)
Palmer's Sixth Form College, Grays

Alone

This girl lived on a planet of joy, happiness
But a cloud of sadness, tragedy concealed the sun's vibrant rays
Her world had become a bitter planet of isolation
No warmth, no love
Just ignorance... just darkness
They would perform an act of care, kindness
It was just an act, an act
She evaluated in her mind
They smile but they do not know, they embrace but they do not feel
They will never know, they will never feel
Unless that cloud destroyed their sun, their stars, their moon
Yet she didn't let the cloud take over
Despite everything, she didn't let it take over
For it only remained for a while
It felt like hours, years, but it was only for a while
The girl was surrounded by many
They were kind, understanding and meant every word they uttered
Every syllable
She heard the same whisper every day, 'We can do it, we can get through this.'
And as she faced to conquer the world
She looked both left and right
She saw many people on either side
People among people, among people

They were all there to reassure her
They had no weapons, nothing
Just hope
Suddenly, her eyes opened,her ears could only hear hospital machines beeping all around her
A fuzzy figure approached the blurry figures who were sitting beside her
All she heard was, 'I'm sorry, but it's too late.'
She opened her mouth to speak, 'It's OK, I'm not afraid and you shouldn't be either
Thank you for all that you have done for me
I will see you in the next world.'
Her eyes gently closed and she whispered the same words
Over and over again, 'I'm not afraid... I'm not afraid.'

Zara Yurtseven (12)
Palmers Green High School, London

Tollieday

Hello, roll-up, it's time for the Tollieday
A date so incredible it should be a holiday
So sit back and relax; there's no shoving or yelling
Just be carried along by the story I'm telling

My name is Tolani and today I am twelve
I am incredibly pretty, I am ferociously bright
But sometimes the mess in my room is a terrible sight
For, whilst you may marvel at all the books on my shelves
I have a secret identity who dances with elves

I excel at detection, I love Sherlock Holmes
And I solved the case of 'The Mystery Gnomes'
The gnomes had gone missing, they couldn't be seen
And the culprit or culprits had fled from the scene

But what sort of person would plot such a devious crime?
Who'd take the trouble, who'd have the time?
I scoured the neighbourhood looking for clues
I searched the kitchens and bathrooms and examined shoes
And that's when it struck me, all those paw prints on floors
He was the guilty one, it was Boss Cat from next door!

He'd seen gnomes by a pond and thought, *hang on
They're stealing my fish. Do these creatures not know
That sardines are my dish*
So he picked up the gnomes and painted them green
Then hid them in grass where they couldn't be seen

So as you can see, my mind is first rate
But I've got dozens of hobbies, so many things on my plate
Now, it won't be exhaustive, there's too much to relate
But the rest of this poem will put forward and state
Just a few of the things that make Tollie great

Well, let's start with the obvious and mention gymnastics
My body's is bendy most people believe I'm elastic
I've been employing my skills to play hide-and-seek
Against poor uncle Christy who couldn't find me for weeks!
Or how about this, I've ridden a horse
Was I good do you say? Ridiculous question, I was amazing of course

Now that I'm twelve, I've joined senior school
An institution which surely one day soon, I'll just rule
When talking of school, one has to mention careers
A subject which brings all but the bravest parents to tears
But there's no need to worry, there's nothing to fear
Just a poet who lacks the requisite skill and the time
To think of a way to make immunology rhyme

I need to apologise for the state of this verse
It's abundantly clear that I haven't rehearsed
And for the scoundrels insisting that this poem's too long
Rest assured and be thankful, I'll try not tarry long

I'm reaching the end now, I'll try to be terse
With what I'm feeling quite certain is my penultimate verse
My fingers are aching and my memory's tired
And what's even worse, my brain's becoming unwired

So that's what I've written to celebrate T-day
As historically significant as the Normandy Landings on D-Day
I'm finishing now and I'll send you my love
With a flourish of penmanship and thousands of doves.

Tolani Aradeon (12)
Palmers Green High School, London

I'm Okay...

When someone says I'm okay
They're really holding back tears
You are their worst of fears
You push her down
And make her frown
But she still says, 'I'm okay.'
They're really living in a constant nightmare
How is this fair?
You call her fat
And all that
But guess what she does at home?
She's constantly on her phone
Trying to find some diet pills
Yet she still says, 'I'm OK.'
You stamp on her foot
But guess what?
She's already been abused in the past
So she covers her scars like she's wearing a mask
But she still says, 'I'm OK.'
Months have passed
She wants to stop and live the dream when that day is the last
So she runs to the kitchen
Opens the drawer
She can't take it no more!
She searches and searches

And finds what she calls a prize
The sharp blade stares back into her eyes
She places it on her arm
Is this the start of self-harm?
But she still says, 'I'm OK...'

Madison Allen (12)
Queensmead School, London

True Friends

Before you become a friend of mine,
We knew each other for quite some time,
I hate to say we wasted a year and a half,
I'm glad we can now look back and laugh,
It's funny how things turned out,
I wish I could say I never had a doubt,
Truth is, I'm proud to say,
You and I have come a long, long way,
You touch the lives of people you know,
You walk around with a humble glow
You've been a best friend to me,
One that will last for eternity.

I know my secrets, you will keep,
On your shoulder I can weep,
You always listen and never judge me,
You always understand so objectively,
You light up a room when you walk in,
I'm so fortunate that you're my friend,
You are the essence of a best friend,
I wish I had known that way back then,
I'm thankful it was not too late,
My friendship with you was well worth the wait,
I love you for all that you are,
There's no better friend by far.

Noor Shah (11)
Queensmead School, London

Shed That Fear

Shed that fear that you wear and you could find yourself
About to jump the Burj Khalifa.
You're thinking please,
I could live in the jungle with nothing but a pear!
I'm more volcanic than a tufa.

Shed that fear that you wear and you could find yourself
Stepping out of your comfort zone,
Trying something new.
You will have blown the world away,
And you know it too.

Shed that fear that you wear and you will see
Who you really are,
Shining brighter than the other 'stars'.
I know you can do it by doing what you do.
Surely, you can get there by simply being you.
Never let anyone change this.
Remember: if there is only one of you in the entire world
Why not just embrace yourself?

Eiman Ali (12)
Queensmead School, London

Soul

A child is a soul
That can't even break
It's even harder than coal
For heaven's sake
Just take a moment
To breathe in these words
Because all of them want to fly free like birds

Some kids have to share
All they want is fresh air
But they love to care
For one like that might
Just might
See the light
One day

Do you ever feel in your life
That you want to get a knife
But everyone around you will just stare
Because they all think the same
They all think you're lame
But that doesn't matter
Just let them chatter

They can't change your soul
Because like I said, it's harder than coal
That can't ever break
Just let your tears

Run down a lake
Until it all clears
And be yourself!

Soul.

Hewa Hassan (11)
Queensmead School, London

Cycles

The cycle of life, the cycle of death
Each fruit becomes ripe
Each dragon has breath
Those who fight for freedom, those who wage war
Each king has a kingdom, open the house door
All cycles are the same

But there's one exception, it's very dark
It brings pain like a caged lark
It varies, depending on hate
They're corrupted, and can't say, 'Yo mate.'
Stamp out this one, and fill it with fun
Every cycle repeats itself

It's fascinating, there are so many
You try to count, but can't see any
The universe of cycles is unique
In its own way

Peter Connell (11)
Queensmead School, London

How Is It Fair?

How is it fair
That lives are to spare
For great leaders argue
Whether whoever the land should go to

How is it fair
That in Africa people struggle to survive
And all the way in Syria bombs arrive
From US, Russia, Britain and all sorts

How is is fair
That people are sent to court
For things they didn't do
Whilst children hardly find food to chew

Their mum works minimum wage
Because their Christian boss doesn't like her Muslim face
But her Jewish friend gets paid extra
This isn't the way to grade

How is this fair?

Leina Marhoum (11)
Queensmead School, London

If Only

If only they could see the things she's going through
If only, if only, if only they knew
If only they wouldn't pick on her every day
Because all she wants is to learn and play
If only everyday she didn't feel worried and sick
If she had the choice to come into school what do you think she'd pick
If only, if only no one knew all her fears
You could fill another River Thames with that amount of tears
If only, if only they could see her smile
Maybe not all the time, just once in a while

Francesca Tully (11)
Queensmead School, London

Abandoned Dogs

One day in May
I found a dog
I wanted to play
But he was stuck in a bog
I had to help him out
But he was really stuck
I found a stick by a bin
I used it to help him up

I took him to the vet to find the chip
It turned out that he was no ones pet
Other than that he lived in a skip
I let him sleep in my perfect bed
I gave him lots of love and care
After the terrible ordeal
I found a comfy sweater for him to wear
I adopted him and now he's in good care

Randeep Bhachu (12)
Queensmead School, London

Summer

When my mum opens my bright yellow curtains
My dark brown eyes start to squint quickly
I feel the hot, thin air steaming up
When is summer going to end?

After the bright morning we went to the busy beach
I hear the cute little birds tweeting with happiness
Rosy red flowers explode in black
At yellow stripy bees devouring the pollen

Suddenly the dull night sky awakens
And the humid air cools
Everyone sighs with relief
And the angry waves stop bashing

Swika Srikanth (11)
Queensmead School, London

The Sea

The sea is blue, as blue as you
This is the sea, the wavy sea
There are fish swimming and twirling
And spinning and singing happily in the sea
Dolphins dancing and whales singing all happy at the sea
Oh what a beautiful place to live
This is the sea, the happy sea

Aïsha Mancero (11)
Queensmead School, London

I Is Me

How great it is to be me!
I am who I am from the beginning to be
I roam the Earth in this body you see
For me is I and I am me!
How lovely it is to have my eyes
That hold the big, brown circles inside
That see things dumb, old and wise
How lovely it is to have my eyes
What a great gift to have my skin
Who cares what colour it holds within
Each single hair, long and thin
What holds within is my skin
And beware my hands, they do not lie
They write each verse, they try and try
To comfort your friend if they cry
They do not lie, my hands and I
And my tongue, oh my tongue
The story it tells
The simple greetings, hello to farewell
The words from my tongue, they treat you well
And who cannot forget my feet
Each little piggy holds a treat
From stinky and messy to rosy and neat
Hello little piggies, hello my feet
How great it is to be me!
I am who I am from the beginning to be

I roam the Earth in this body you see
For me is I and I am me!

Isabella Soremi (11)
St Bernard's High School, Westcliff-On-Sea

Strengths

Everyone has strengths
Everyone's strength is different
Because everyone is unique
And nothing is the same
Nothing is normal

Elephants as big as they are
And mice as small as they are
Are all special to the world, their herd or their mischief
Their family and friends
The eco system is balanced by everyone's strengths
In the sea
Whales and clownfish
Big and small
Everything and everyone is special

Elephants have the strength of memory
And mice have the strength of stealth
But that doesn't mean the mouse is inferior
Because it is small
And whales have the strength to jump above the surface of the water
And clownfish are immune to the venom of the anemone
But that doesn't mean the whale's strength is far greater than the clownfish

Like the animals we all have strengths too
May it be the obvious ones like:
Science, English, maths or performing arts
Or is it the abstract ones such as:
You are good at sharing joy
You are good at making choices
Or do you have an interest in world peace?
These are the qualities of everyone
The qualities of each individual person
These different qualities are what we all should admire.

Emma Alston (12)
St John The Baptist School, Woking

Choices

Choices are options, choices are friends, choices are the little things we never seem to think much of
They can be joy and they can be pain
However no matter their size, their importance is beyond measure

Choices are thoughts, they are big and small
From marriage or friends down to books or balls
Choices are puzzles because they never seem to be complete
Choices are people just waiting to meet
Choices are banks of thoughts, rich or not
Each choice can cost and risk a lot

They are never going to stop, they're here forevermore
Each thought, each smile, each treat and each hesitation
They just water the plant that is never fully grown
The more water it has, the bigger it gets
But don't let the plant get too big and don't let it drown

Don't feed
Choices too much thought
But don't let them walk away
With none

Remember
The choices you made yesterday
Do they lead you here?

Because in the end
We only regret the decisions we didn't make
And the chances we never took...

Georgia Evans (12)
St John The Baptist School, Woking

Everyone Is Different

There are many different types of people
They have different personalities, different hobbies and they are all unique
There are those who are easy-going and enjoy a bit of sewing
And there are those who like prancing or just plain dancing
There are the ones who are like Denis who like to play tennis
But one thing's for sure, they are all different.

Some wear hats, others flats
Ties are often seen, where others dress smart and pristine
Most are tall lengthwise, and the remaining? They are pint-sized
But that is okay, because everyone is different.

There are many people in this world
Those who are brave lions, or the gentlest of dandelions
The bunnies, meek and the cheetahs, sleek
Some are like two peas in a pod
And some, they rule the squad
But who is to judge them, everyone is different.

Charlotte Saul (12)
St John The Baptist School, Woking

Moving

At first it's a lot to take right in
One day you're there and now you're here
I have travelled overseas recently from my parents' home country Zimbabwe
It occurs to me that my life has changed
I have to start all over
I miss my friends and family
And the memories that I have made

I've met many pleasant people
Who have shown me the ways of life here in the UK
And I feel I'm starting to fit in
I have to say Zimbabwe will forever stay in my heart and close to me
But for now I will be fine keeping in mind that God is forever with me

Shona Ndoro (12)
St John The Baptist School, Woking

The Wild Race

We are all stood on a line
I am stood next to some friends of mine
My legs are shaking whilst my confidence is breaking
My heart is beating harder than a drum
I am thinking to myself, *this won't be fun*
The coach is exclaiming, 'Who is ready to run?'
I can see the other runners wheezing
My legs are freezing
I can smell the freshly cut grass along with damp mud
I can hear the runners before us screaming
Their faces are more red than blood and they're steaming hot
Will I enjoy this? I think not

Suddenly their coach yells, 'Get ready, get steady.'
He pulls the trigger of the blank gun, now everyone begins to run
Dashing, flashing, bashing together
Everyone wants place number one
We all run packed together as a herd like wolves or even birds
As we go flying up hills and down hills faster than lightning
Everyone fighting to get ahead of the pack
Leaving all the others behind their back

It is a wild race
I better keep up my pace

Also trying not to trip up my shoe lace
My head is sweating but I'm not letting anybody pass me
Not even if they ask nicely

Look, there's the finish line
I'm not running, I'm now jumping to keep up with a friend of mine
I am rushing and rushing to end this race
Whilst the wind is brushing against my face
I crossed the line
Just on time
I won

Joshua Abernethy (11)
St Mary's College, Southampton

Billy The Bully

I remember his face
Too close to mine
I remember the place
And the same old line

A bully is two-faced
Dr Jekyll and Mr Hyde
A school is two-placed
A harbour and landslide

'People like you don't belong,' a boy said
'There are names for your kind.'
So he called me a million, each one held dread
I was verbally stabbed and left for dead

They called me names like fairy
I looked in the mirror, I thought, *that can't be true, I'm just dark and hairy*
They called me a queen, but I'm too handsome and mean to be a queen.

Mia Manreet Kaur Rai (11)
St Mary's College, Southampton

Goodbyes

I never really realised
What goodbyes actually mean
I never counted the moments
They've all gone and been
And when there is that day
Where I have to let you go
I suddenly lose someone precious
Until all that's left is their star glow
My tears become a waterfall
My aching heart is shattered glass
With my mind becoming a passageway
Leading to the past
I know you watch down on me as an angel
But I never really had a clue
That when I said my last goodbyes
I was never again going to get the chance
To say hello to you.

Eleanor Smith (11)
St Mary's College, Southampton

Killer Clowns!

Blood dripping down their face
As they wander round the place
Their lifeless stare
Will give you quite a scare
When they chase you round a bend
They don't want to be your friend!
They tap softly on your window
Jump crazily on your car
You whisper, 'Oh no!'
As they drag you somewhere far
Woken in a graveyard and what do you see?
A pair of killer clowns laughing... hee, hee, hee!

Inas Kassim (11)
St Mary's College, Southampton

The Beautiful Game

Football is like a life cycle
It's a round object repeating itself over and over
For some, it's a matter of life and death
Glory, passion, victory, success, revenge
It has it all
You win; you're a hero to fans
You lose; you're an enemy to fans
Work hard and be at the top...

Will King (11)
St Mary's College, Southampton

Untitled

Being strong and being brave
Being a fighter and being a hero
Being the muscle and picking yourself up when you fall
Thinking of the present and dismissing the past
Is being strong being brave?
Just because you fight does that make you a hero?
Can you pick yourself up with no muscle?
Maybe I don't want to be strong
I don't have to be brave
I'm tired of fighting
Tired of picking myself up
Focussing only on past events
Scared of the future
Having the weight on my shoulders
Too heavy to lift off
Soldiering on
Not having help
But I want help and I need help
I don't want another day to be the same as the last
I want to change
But change is what I am scared of
Horrified of what events will occur if change never takes place
Hiding from what shouldn't be hidden from
Not facing the fears that can be faced
Is that who I will become and always be if change never arrives

Is that who I will stay as if change is never present
I want change
But I can't have it
Can't make it happen
I can't do it
I just can't do it
But if I believe
Yet believing is what I fear
Not raising the expectations too high
Nor being let down
Not losing hope but never having it in the first pace
Seeing the light at the end
Breathing a breath of fresh air
Reaching out for the hand and grabbing it
The lights getting dimmer
The air is getting humid
The hand is slipping away
That miniscule bit of hope getting that much smaller
The fear growing that much bigger

Maddi Davis (12)
Steyning Grammar School, Steyning

Good Friends

Starting school as a happy four-year-old
With friends from my pre-school; we just had fun.
Laughter and learning, doing what we're told
In the classroom, on the field, playing in the sun.

Then there was bullying, came out of nowhere.
The teachers never listened, excuses made.
A few friends protected me, gave me hugs.
Mum challenged the school, I was afraid.

One year left, but I couldn't go on.
A house move, change of school, more nerves for me.
A whole new experience, girls who cared.
I started learning again with smiles you could see.

My confidence soared, school was fun again.
End of year performance - I sang a solo part.
Feeling strong, feeling a part of things, chances to shine.
Parties, equals and girls with a heart.

Now I'm in secondary school - so much has changed.
Being brave enough to say a speech - not once but twice.
Enjoying things that I couldn't consider two years before.
Having fun, learning so much, no hate, being nice.

What a difference good friends can make
In all aspects of your world.
They heal your pain, make you brave,
Make you happy, a sunny future unfolds…

Zoe Ainsworth (11)
Steyning Grammar School, Steyning

I'll Always Be Waiting

I stood ever-waiting the sight of my dear friend, I'll always be waiting
I heard the loud tick of the public clock and counted the ticks in my head
One, two, three, four, five, six, seven, it's been a long time, I'll always be waiting
My eyes were straining from the amount of searching for something I wasn't even sure would come
My legs shook from the amount of standing and waiting, waiting, waiting, I'll always be waiting
As my heart came to a near stop and as my last breath filled the cold air
I lay in what felt like flowers soft as a pillow, I'll always be waiting
My last thought was filled with the empty loneliness that I experienced - the past lifetime
And in what seemed the shortest of time felt myself drift from the galaxy itself
I'll always be waiting
And I see the destination which to me was beyond the scale of beautifulness
But suddenly I felt an immense force pull me back, like I was being sucked into a black hole,
I'll always be waiting
I awoke to the sight of my dear friend who said just one thing, 'I knew I'd find you...'

Cameron Stevens (12)
Steyning Grammar School, Steyning

Sister

You're so special
I look up to you, and when you're not here there's nothing to do
We all love your boyfriend
You're one of a kind
And when we play hide-and-seek you're really hard to find
You're very protective over me
Which is good to see
And when I'm feeling down in the dumps
You tap me on the knee
When you moved to Canterbury I cried my eyes out Holly
But when you came back to see us you made me feel all jolly
Even when we argue we don't really care
Because you and I, we both see we have a lot to share
I've seen you when you're happy
I've seen you when you're sad
But when I watched you cry, oh I felt so bad
I really need you in my life
But you probably don't see that you are just so special
You mean a lot to me
You always make me laugh
You are just so funny

Or when you saved that rabbit and it looked like it was a bunny
No, I'm only joking, it was actually a wild one
But you Holly, are just so full of fun

Thea Hayes (12)
Steyning Grammar School, Steyning

Beach Hut

A little white beach hut sits up on a hill,
The seagulls all roost there; their voices are shrill.
The paint is a-peeling, it's stood there for years,
It misses the sun, the smiles and the tears.

The long summer days before wasting away,
It wishes that then in the past it could stay.
It tried at the door but the hinges have rusted,
It looks through the roof which couldn't be trusted.

A little white beach hut sits up on a hill,
Unaware of the writing inscribed on the will.

Perhaps his last words will be carried out still.

Oscar Loveridge (12)
Steyning Grammar School, Steyning

My Reliable Friend

My life was miserable
Until I met you
My lies would keep going
But you made me stop

With all of the trouble I have
You get me through them all
And not being able to slow down
You help me stop them all

Because lying is bad
And I want to stop
But sometimes I can't
This person helps me to stop

But now I finally stopped
All thanks to this person
I have finally stopped
And I love her for this

Alfie Baxter (12)
Steyning Grammar School, Steyning

Imagine The Opposite

I sit here, in front of my computer, warm and content in this cosy, comforting room
Its warmth surrounds me like an invisible blanket
As I stare up happily at the moon
Imagine the opposite
I lie here cold, and hungry, on this thread-bare woollen carpet
In this freezing, dank and musty space
My breath condensing into a cloud of fear
Slowly, salty pearls of sadness drip down my face

Daniel McGuire (12)
Steyning Grammar School, Steyning

Whistling Wind

The birds sing like whistling wind
The wolves howl like the whistling wind
Everything, everyone enjoys the whistling wind
The whistling wind is our home
The whistling wind is our life
The whistling wind hands us living supplies
The whistling wind gives us hope
The whistling wind is our home
We are the whistling wind's pets
We are the animals in the forest

Jade Hodges (11)
Steyning Grammar School, Steyning

I'll Remember You

I'll remember you
You left when I was five
I've remembered you since 2009
I never cried when I was with you
Until it came to 2009
You picked me up like I was flying
And called me Zumo all the morning
You gave me a red bag and my sister the blue
I will always remember you

Sophie Martin (12)
Steyning Grammar School, Steyning

Flying In The Sky

Flying in the sky
So very, very high
Soaring with the birds up there
Seeing everything everywhere

Flitter like a butterfly
Buzzing like a bee
Everything is beautiful, so beautiful to see
Flying, flying very high
Flying in the sky

Katie Ward (13)
Steyning Grammar School, Steyning

My Mum

My mum likes to take me shopping
Although I'd rather not
She takes so long in every store
She seems to buy a lot
But I love my mum

She makes me walk to Waitrose
Which really is quite far
I have to carry home two bags
Because we have no car
But I love my mum

My mum says I must drink more milk
So that I will grow
I really do not like it
Yet she ignores my, 'No!'
But I love my mum

I'm told to clean my bedroom
It is a boring job
She knows I'm clearly busy
This make me want to sob
But I love my mum

I know I eat so slowly
But it's better to digest
I'm always told to hurry up
Although I do my best
But I love my mum

She says I'm always on my phone
But I don't think that's true
I'm looking at important things
I'm sure that's what I do
But I love my mum

When I'm trying to do my homework
My mum keeps butting in
'Do this, do that,' she always says
Making such a din
But I love my mum

I know that my mum loves me
Although it's left unsaid
She gives me such a loving smile
When she tucks me up in bed
I love my mum

Fay Burbery (11)
The Folkestone School For Girls, Folkestone

Tales From The Sea

An inky tail drifted past
Underwater every moment lasts
A scaly fin turned round to swipe
The leafy coral to my right

Her hair waved down to her waist
A few stray flowers kept it in place
A couple of bubbles floated through the sea
They whispered tales of mystery
Of sad sea men on worn out boats
And true love that they never spoke

Although there were a few blue fish
The sea was empty of the right dish
She swam up to a plant
And picked it off although she can't
Make a meal from seaweed
Only from krill and algae
But where she will find it is the question
The others offered the suggestion
Go deeper, you'll find your food
And maybe this time the right dude

She followed what they said and swam down to the deep
Passing a few jellyfish on her way to meet
Her lover so dear that waited patiently
Sitting on the rock singing songs from the sea
He wore a beaded necklace with bone and rope

That he passed to his mermaid the next time they spoke
But she lost it so tragic although the next bit is pure magic
I was walking along the golden sand
When I found the beaded necklace lying patiently
For the new owner to arrive so it could spin tales of the sea...

Erin Gregory (11)
The Folkestone School For Girls, Folkestone

The Silent Dancer

Each strand of hair on my arm rises
Welcoming the dainty melody
The gentle tones build up into a tune
Captivating my entire body.
The calming music whispers
And its loving arms embrace
Gently stroke my shaking hands
Bringing confidence and colour to my face.

My shaking, nervous hands
Trembling, shuddering with trepidation
Are held by the warming hands of music
Removing every ounce of apprehension.
The trace of confidence from deep within
Gains determination, strength and power
And all emotion that has built up inside
Eventually emerges from its ivory tower.

Released from the confinements of anxiety
My hands become my restrained voice
Expressing myself through gentle gestures
I display happiness, love and rejoice.
The floor is my canvas, blemished by each twirl
Painted upon my worn-out ballet shoes
Is now a masterpiece of emotions
And is indented, scratched and bruised.

The words which I cannot express
The emotions which I feel
Upon the sound of a single tune
Can all finally be revealed.
A voice trapped within a box
Silent, useless, under a trance
Expression is bound by everything
For me but when I dance.

Aimee McCarthy (12)
The Folkestone School For Girls, Folkestone

Depression

Depression eats you up inside
It forces you to forget what being happy feels like
It drives you to insanity
Anyone can get it
And anyone can cause it
From society pressuring people to be perfect
To someone commenting on your large nose
Or your body fat
Or just the fact you have braces
It could even just be the fact that you're stressed with work piling up
Or being home on time so your family won't get worried
It can be caused by anxiety or insomnia.
Anything.
It may not be a physical disease
But it still has the power to kill anyone
That is until you finally find someone or something
It could be how passionate actors are
The way your friends cheer you up
The fact that your family will never stop loving you
When dance allows you to express yourself in every way
Or how music can be your one release
Any little thing that makes an immense difference

That defeats the bleak, once-unbeatable depression
Because some people may not have enough time to find this small difference
But it's always there.

Charlotte Hastie (13)
The Folkestone School For Girls, Folkestone

I'm No Different To You

As I wander round town, eyes stop and stare
Calling me names cos my skin isn't fair
Inside I'm no different so why do you say
That you're better than me in many a way

Whenever I'm out for my safety I fear
My faith causes people to violently cheer
Vigorous language is fired at me
Why should I feel like I always must flee?

I hear them discuss what they think is wrong with me
Being alienated because I need glasses to see
But who should determine the way I should look
It's just like judging the front of a book

From inside to out their words tear me apart
To describe how I feel brokenness is a start
Oh my heart screams with pain how I wish things would change
Why is everyone calling me strange?

If only the world could brighten its view
To be joyful and happy, that would be something new
Don't single out differences, rejoice them instead
My wish is that the world could be equally led

Katelyn Mae Rawlings (12)
The Folkestone School For Girls, Folkestone

Dreamer

I am a dreamer that never stops dreaming
I wonder what comes tomorrow
I hear words running around my mind
I see the future, big and bold
I want so many kids and to live forever
I am a dreamer that never stops dreaming.

I pretend that I have no fears
I feel love and heartbreak
I touch the hearts of others
I worry that I'm not good enough
I cry in my mind and show it sometimes
I am a dreamer that never stops dreaming.

I understand that some people don't get me
I say less than my thoughts say
I dream big and beautiful
I try to impress
I hope that the world never ends
I am a dreamer that never stops dreaming.

I dream these things night after night
I can't stop these cruel thoughts
I over think things a lot
I hope these things last forever
I dream again and again
I am a dreamer that never stops dreaming.

Zoe Emma Hillman (12)
The Folkestone School For Girls, Folkestone

Pow!

A bullet lost along with a life
You can't compare the sacrifice
Uncles, fathers, brothers galore
All sucked into the tornado of war

No one really knew what would become
But they no longer jumped at the sound of a gun
Imagine wishing day after day
That it would not be your loved one
Another man's prey

Waiting, waiting, to hear your fate
Life is too big of a gift to donate
Like a volcano, war causes eruption
Bubbling, bubbling until it causes destruction

War creeps in like a disease
One that you can't escape
And all that is left is memories
Ones you can't recreate

Each day is a gift itself
And each shot is a threat
No padding, guns, shields or swords
Really can protect

Cleaning, scrubbing, working, wishing
Creates their day to day life
And all they have to lean on is hope
Their rock, through all their strife

Molly Harding (11)
The Folkestone School For Girls, Folkestone

Peculiar Skies

There was a peculiar sound
In the sky
First a rumble then a jumble
Silence!

I turned and faced the sky
The clouds were shallow grey
Yet the grass was green and bright

I held my head high hoping to
Catch a glimmer of light
But there was nothing
Nothing seized my attention
Apart from the growling cloud above

The sun had gone into hiding resting peacefully
From using up all its might
I thought to myself and wondered
What would happen if the sun had no might?

No plants would grow
No dazzling rainbows
No sunny days at the beach
No delicious ice cream treats

No playing in the warm sea
No dancing at the beach
No atmosphere
No light

These are possibilities that no one
really considers, but maybe they would
if only they knew what the world could do
So be considerate of peculiar skies

Emma Lowther (12)
The Folkestone School For Girls, Folkestone

Life With Depression

Depression is a war
A battle against yourself
Every thought is a bullet
Every movement is a punch
Every word is a stab in the heart
Depression is a thief
It steals everything you once had
Everything left behind you keep trapped
Depression is a murderer
You look in the mirror
And you see this thing
Depression is a zombie
You're alive but you're dead
You're the walking dead
Depression is a nightmare
You wake up into a hell
You're afraid of living
Everything seems impossible to bear
Depression is an ocean
A sea of emotion
You're dreaming every day
But you're never saved
Depression is a bottomless pit
Never-ending pain
Never-ending struggles
There is no light

There is no escape
Depression is a war
A battle against yourself
Depression is a war
You either win
Or you die trying

Chlóe Wallace (12)
The Folkestone School For Girls, Folkestone

Ballerina Shine

We are all ballerinas
Tying our broken, battered toes
Into pretty satin slippers
Complete with pink little bows

All I ever do is practise
Coming to the studio to train
It's my fault though because I love it
No one else can take the blame!

But there are others, better, stronger than me
So sometimes I don't get a chance to shine
Pirouetting, twirling, bending backwards
Maybe it isn't my time

Sticks and stones won't break our bones
But injuries come and go
We go up on pointe to the tip top
The music makes our moves flow

Now on the stage we're dancing
Looking out to the crowd
One day my name will be up there in lights
And I hope I make people proud

We are all ballerinas
Tying our broken, battered toes
Into pretty satin slippers
Wondering which way our life will go

Lydia Stanton (12)
The Folkestone School For Girls, Folkestone

Life's Better At The Beach

On a summer's day; life is better at the beach...
Glistening blue sea, washing up the sandy shore
The guardian angel flashing its comforting light to passing ships
Squawking seagulls gliding delicately
Life's better at the beach

Candy coloured beach huts lined elegantly along the promenade
Buckets and spades clutter the golden sand
Sun-kissed children building their forts with fun-filled enjoyment
Interrupted by the jolly sound of ice cream
Life's better at the beach

Abandoned rock pools appear to be explored, left by the magical seas
Crabs and fish attempt to scarper whilst avoiding the little one's nets
Soggy seaweed draped alongside the intricate, discarded shells
The shimmering sun in our eyes, wet sand between our toes, our day's an adventure
Life's better at the beach

Niamh Emily Simmons (12)
The Folkestone School For Girls, Folkestone

You're Different

Racism: a form of discrimination to people of a different race
That's an understatement
Racism is a group of people who don't accept the fact there is difference
They stare at you and whisper about your skin colour or religion
You try and fight for your rights but your point will never be put across
That is what racism is
People who don't accept difference
Everyone is different whether it's skin, race or size
What world would this be without difference?
Same people eating the same thing, doing the same thing
Playing the same thing
How boring is that?
Difference says you want change so if people make fun of your skin, race or size
Ignore them because you're different and that's what makes you who you are
You're different and be proud of it

Eksha Chongbang (12)
The Folkestone School For Girls, Folkestone

The Four Seasons

All four seasons
Different times of the year
Sun, wind, rain
How different they appear

Spring is a time for new life
Lots of animals are born
Many plants start to grow
The farmers plant their corn

In summer I like to go to the beach
The sun caresses my skin
Swimming, surfing, sandcastles too
Any competition, I will win

In autumn animals hibernate
As the weather goes cool
Harvest comes, farmers dig up their crops
And the colourful leaves all fall

Winter brings the festive period
Christmas is when family is together
Everyone is generous and kind
All jolly despite the weather

All four seasons
Different times of the year
Sun, wind, rain
How different they appear

Chloe Wiggins (12)
The Folkestone School For Girls, Folkestone

World Without Us

Life when it began
All animals, all trees, all wildlife
Nothing destroyed, nothing hurt

Seasons perfect
All snow, all sun, all rain
Nothing destroyed, nothing hurt

It was peaceful
All in harmony, all in peace
Nothing destroyed, nothing hurt

Then they came
All forests cut, all fruit picked
Nothing left, all gone

Their humongous machines tore us apart
All eaten, all poisoned
Nothing left, all gone

They became smarter and smarter
Populations grew bigger and bigger
More babies born, more houses built
More habitats lost, more animals gone
Nothing left, all gone

How smart do humans need to be, to stop begin stupid?

Sienna Lukey (12)
The Folkestone School For Girls, Folkestone

To Dance

My toes snuggly cramped in my shoes so tight,
I nervously step forward to impress.
Sweaty palms, a damp brow, let's get this right.

Standing tall, arms straight and stiff, hair quiffed,
Just me, three judges and my dream.
I spin, kick and click.

Crystals on my dress radiantly reflect,
Six eyes deciding my fate.
Forty bars of dance; I'm wrecked.
Music stops, I politely bow.

Results time arrives and my heart is pounding,
a cup would be welcome, my confidence is wavering.

From thirty-four down to two, champion is who?
The judges say, 'You!'
Not born in Ireland, but born to dance in it
Triumphantly, I struggle to lift my trophy.

Harriett Fleur Harper (12)
The Folkestone School For Girls, Folkestone

Bullies

People can be like animals
Some hide inside a shell
Some leap about
And sing and shout
And let their feelings out

When people try to hide
Whatever they are feeling inside
You could often hurt them without them showing
But people could do it on purpose or even without knowing

Now hurt and pain can come in different ways
Physical, emotional, cyber and verbal
But all of these people shouldn't be circled
By bullies and other kinds of people
They should have space and be able to share all opinions

Now no matter what people say or do
There is one word
Which you should learn
Which is...
Safe
Meet
Accepting
Reliable
Tell

Emily Rose Harlow (11)
The Folkestone School For Girls, Folkestone

A Summer's Day

I'm waiting eagerly for summer
To come around
Sitting down, lounging around
Listening to my music sounds

Finally it has come at last
Don't know what to do but it's gonna be a blast
Swimming, jumping, having a great time

Splash, boom, wish this could be real life
Ice cold freezing pop
Eating swiftly up the lot
Climbing, jumping, playing games
Oh how I love this summer day

Hot sun beating down
Sweating and sun-lounging all around
BBQ roasting, flame fire
What could make this day any higher?

The sun goes in
We all cave in
For summer is over
No one to wonder

Lillian Watts (12)
The Folkestone School For Girls, Folkestone

It's Up To You

A horse is the refection of your soul
A mirror to your emotions
If a horse comes, it's because of you
If a horse leaves, it's because of you

You could ride him through the leaves
Jump him over logs
The horse might come, it's up to you
But if the horse leaves, it's because of you

You could groom him when it's sunny
Or brush him when it's stormy
If the horse comes, it's because of you
Or he might leave, it's up to you

The horse, a reflection of your soul
You rode him, you jumped him
You groomed him, you brushed him
The horse came, because of you

Ella Louise Russell (12)
The Folkestone School For Girls, Folkestone

The Big Race

My name is called, I look around me
My heart thundering in my chest
Feel like I'm suffocating
Beads of sweat appear on my forehead
My palms are sweaty, knees weak
My eyes fixed on the line, I take my position
On your marks, sounds distant
Get set, sounds like I'm underwater
Go! I spring up, legs strong
Feel the adventure kick in
The cold air in my face whistling
Past my ears, pushing, pushing
Done it, finished, crossed the line
Looking around me, exhaustion
Taking over my body, nerves
Tingling, breathing hard, wait
I won, the joy, the relief, the cheer.

Macey Forster (13)
The Folkestone School For Girls, Folkestone

Racism

Black or white
Blue eyes or brown eyes
Netball or dance
What's the difference?

If you don't say it about eye colour
Then why the skin colour
Racism is as bad as a crime
So why discriminate?

It's nobody's choice
Everyone is different
There's no need for it
So what makes you do it?

How would you like it?
This is a serious matter
Just because they're different
That is no excuse

If we were all the same
The world would be a different place
But not for the good
For the bad

Sophie Ida Shield (12)
The Folkestone School For Girls, Folkestone

Memories

My memories of this person I think about a lot
And they all began at a very special spot
Playing in the garden
Swinging on the swings
Doing all imaginative things

My memories of this place will never be forgotten
Collecting all the apples that soon went rotten
Water in the bird bath so we had fed them
And listening to the radio
Pennies from Heaven

My memories of this home will always be with me
Yet little did I know
One day it would be empty
The last time we did our 'mwah, mwah' kiss
I will always and forever cherish and miss

Isobella Church (11)
The Folkestone School For Girls, Folkestone

Society

Society's horrible
People expect you to look good
We get left out if we don't
But we are all different

We get called names
We get bullied
We get hurt
Just because we are all different

You don't expect people to care
Every day is a struggle
But we're told to get through it
We are all different

Some of society are thick or thin
Tall or short
Spotty or not
We are all different

We would like to be respected
For who we really are
No hatred
Just because we are all different

Alice Payne (13)
The Folkestone School For Girls, Folkestone

The Dark

What is the dark?
The dark is an ebony blanket
with white dots.
The dark is a leathery hand
ready to kidnap the sun.

What is the dark?
The dark is a person that has
the strength to close the walls on you,
until there isn't any light.
The dark is a criminal mastermind,
who no one can ever catch.

What is the dark?
The dark is your worst nightmare,
silently hiding under your bed.
The dark is really just a black
piece of card with a big white circle.

There is nothing to be afraid of...
Except the dark.

Brooke Marshall (12)
The Folkestone School For Girls, Folkestone

Snowy Paradise

Between my boots, the powdered snow and my slender board,
Ready to tear down the intimidating slopes.
Imagine how I could soar,
my heart's thumping as I gaze, as my fellow boarders elope.

As speed pulls me, twisting and turning around the bends,
My heel edge slices the ice.
Through the picture perfect trees,
I sit on the lift and absorb my snow paradise.

Nervously anticipating; reaching the peak,
I trap my boots behind the bindings.
I gaze down on the mountain, exhilaration I seek,
the glare of the crystal snow; blinding.

Isy Mae Harper (12)
The Folkestone School For Girls, Folkestone

Insecurity

Everyone's shy
Too scared to show
Too afraid they'll be judged

The aim is to be perfect
But what is perfect?
It's much more than just an adjective
It's a goal

You have to have a good figure
You have to be straight
You have to be something impossible

Social media plays a big part in confidence
All the photoshopped bodies
All the airbrushed faces
All the fakery

But, over all these demands
Why can't we just be ourselves?
It's not that hard, is it?

Hannah Parry (12)
The Folkestone School For Girls, Folkestone

Winter Is Coming

Autumn draws to an end
Leaves fall off the trees
The air turns into a bitter chill
And the pavements start to freeze

Families building their fires
To get their homes toasty and warm
Winter is truly coming
The air thick with blizzards and storms

Children so excited about Christmas
The thoughts of presents and fun
Families and friends reunited
All back together as one

As New Year's will soon be upon us
With fireworks on display
A fresh start for everyone
To wash all the worries away

Freya Bailey (11)
The Folkestone School For Girls, Folkestone

The Horse

A whirl of tail and mane whisked in the air
Thundering hooves on the ground
Muscles heaving
The picture of the horse

Whips and stirrups glistening in the sunlight
Beautiful figures dancing in the gentle breeze
Necks arched and ears pricked
The intelligence of the horse

Dust in the air
Brush against flank
Manes stunningly braided
The beauty of the horse

Galloping around the field
Heads high in the air
Racing round, rearing and bucking
The wildness of the horse

Olivia Woodland-Owen (12)
The Folkestone School For Girls, Folkestone

The Other Day On The Bus

The other day on the bus
The boys they shout and swore
When the driver asked them to hush
The noise was no more

The other day from the bus
The view was such a delight
Inside the bus newspaper is thrown
Ending with a fight

The other day on the bus
It was a very bumpy ride
The pole to hold slipped away
And I began to slide

The other day on the bus
The boys were smelling foul
Until we smelt petrol fumes
And realised we'd broken down!

Lily Miller (13)
The Folkestone School For Girls, Folkestone

Squished And Squashed!

Beady eyes and big, broad hands
Bigger feet to help it stand
No wonder they quiver when they're scared
Many people wouldn't care

If you were tiny, smaller too
Then you would understand as you
Wouldn't like to be squished or squashed
You wouldn't like to witness a tragic loss

So maybe when you're standing there
Take a minute to look, to care
For maybe if you were to see
How hard it is to be a bee

Lily Bryan (11)
The Folkestone School For Girls, Folkestone

Friends!

Friends aren't just people that do things together
They have a friendship that no one understands
They don't just leave
They stick together

Even when times are tough
They remember what's really important
Friendship is more important than anything
They stick together

Friends mean everything
You can go to them whenever
You can tell them anything
They stick together
Everyone deserves a best friend

Ella Carter (11)
The Folkestone School For Girls, Folkestone

Netball

Netball, netball, you're the sport for me
There really is no other sport I'd rather play you see
I may be small, I may be short
However true that may be
That does not stop me playing on the court
You must believe
I run, jump, twist and shout as much as possible
Sometimes, so quickly I run into the wall
You must be fast, you must be smart
You must be able to dart
And once its in the net, you see
We join and hug like me!

Ema Calvo (11)
The Folkestone School For Girls, Folkestone

Sadness

A cold tear ran down my face
When will I ever feel happy?
A life slipped away
Was it worth living?

A cold shiver ran down my spine
My heart beat faster
Why me?
When will it stop?

As the salty tears make me blind
Run into my mouth
All I can feel is a sense of hurtfulness
Why?

Staining my red rosy cheeks
My life waves goodbye to me
Am I broken?
Why sadness?

Carla Fleetwood (12)
The Folkestone School For Girls, Folkestone

Books Are Like Another World

Books can take you to another world
Somewhere you couldn't live without
Books are magical and great

That world is called imagination
The creativity of the mind
It is great for all

Whether it's fantasy
Or a complete mystery
Your mind is still a complete factory

Books can take you to another world
Somewhere you couldn't live without
Books are magical and great

Abbie Conyers (12)
The Folkestone School For Girls, Folkestone

Child With A Story

There he sits
Sits on the cold, hard floor
Floor, revolting and rotting
Rotting house, neglected
Neglected child, neglected dreams
Dreams made impossible
Impossible is a word echoing around his head

Head filled with thoughts
Thoughts become troubled
Troubles becomes a personality description
Descriptions become labels
Labels have to be rewritten

Phoebe Reynolds (12)
The Folkestone School For Girls, Folkestone

The Ocean

It reflects the glowing moonlight
In the middle of the night
It really is a magical sight
Above, the soaring birds take flight

Peacefully it lays still
Still as a brick wall
It flows gently in the wind
Not a single ripple to be seen

Silently, it waves in the breeze
I look at it
It looks back at me
The beautiful sight of the sea

Eve Draper Topping (11)
The Folkestone School For Girls, Folkestone

Stand Out

Be the light,
In the dark.
Be the still,
In the storm.
When all is boring,
Be the weird.
Be the brave,
When all is feared.
Whilst at war,
Help it cease.
And always bring,
Hope and peace.

Natalie Burton (11)
The Folkestone School For Girls, Folkestone

We Dance...

We dance...
We dance for fun
We dance for tears
We dance for the applause
We dance for fears
We are the dancers
And we appear

Georgia Mae Ashman (11)
The Folkestone School For Girls, Folkestone

We're Failing

Do you remember the troublemakers?
In Year 1 and Year 2;
Who kept doing bad things?
So you were punished too.
And the troublemakers you saw;
That the teachers overlooked?
But as soon as you did wrong;
You're forever in the bad book.

Well, that's how Muslims feel.
Every. Single. Day.
When we're blamed for everything.
It's eating me away.

Because when I'm learning history,
Thoughts come in my mind,
About how Jews were treated,
By the Nazi regime,
I compare it to the present,
And realise that all I really see:
Is that people are failing,
To learn from history.

The Holocaust started,
With giving Jews the blame,
For every trouble that occurred,
And then putting them to shame.
Making their race the minority;

Their confidence tear,
When they're like everyone else,
But filled up with more fear.

That was just the beginning,
Before the death of six million Jews.
I would turn back time and stop it,
If I could choose.
Because none of those Jews,
Deserved to have died,
Because a despotic leader,
Thought he had a right:
To isolate a certain race;
And groups he disliked,
Then suffocate them;
Or labour them till they died.

Now since 9/11 in 2001,
Muslims have had a bad name.
Being reminded every day,
Has filled our hearts with shame.

We're asked how we feel,
To be part of a religion:
That killed so many innocents,
But that's not my religion.

So I give apology,
On behalf of the flawed;
Who took away innocent lives,

With the name of my Lord.

To the innocent people,
In Syria and Palestine,
For always getting bombed;
But only remembered time to time.

To the people in Orlando,
In Brussels and Paris;
Although being cared for,
Still being attacked by terrorists.

To the innocent Muslims,
Who have been taken off planes,
For reasons so ignorant,
Foolish and lame.

To my parents and other Muslims,
Who are constantly accused,
By people of the public,
And also racially abused.

It's not only about Muslims;
It's about Mexicans and Blacks.
They're being completely disregarded;
Wish I could say it's a hoax.

'Cause we're living in a world,
Where there are minority races.
And many empty-headed people,
Who want to take this to places:

Kill Muslims with pig blood,
Build walls between places,
Don't let Muslims in America,
Especially those who cover their faces.
Don't let black lives matter,
Send Syrians back to their 'homes',
Put surveillance in mosques,
In case of ISIS-funded phones.

We can't watch this happen.
Stand around and wait.
So open your eyes now;
Before it's way too late.

Hafsa Moolla (15)
Walthamstow School For Girls, London

Captivity

What is war to me?
It is violence
One that drove my family apart
Falling asleep with dry tears on my cheeks
Only to find myself choking on the tears
Like a rusty pipe with a hollow leak
I couldn't fill the pain that echoed
And trembled through my limbs, my blood
Tracing my heart
Just like the fear that stampeded
Through my street, my city
Resting upon my country
A part of me
Through the channel of evil it retreated

What was once a land of grace and beauty
Is now a deserted land of death and sorrow
Now my eyes awaken to the fragments of bones
All the flesh feasted on and demolished
The rest of the world viewed my home as a carcass
No one could stop the beast
No one!

Rape, blood and massacres
Only through power it was unleashed
Now my people, once strong through unity
Have fallen

Their knees trembling brutally
This was the trademark for rights being despoiled
Blood once spilt for sacred rituals, now
Become intertwined with the roots of the soil.

Where were the rights of peace?
They say you're innocent until proven guilty
But my country, she was denied a fair plea
People picturing us barefoot running with kites
But through government they were brainwashed
And with fear and guns my land was hushed
Where's the love that used to run so divine and free?
My native land once bountiful, now hollow as the sea.

If only there was still a Holy shrine
Where God pronounced the happy couple wed
The world and love
Which is now corrupt blood streaming through the veins of the world
Love stood at the altar
Hatred conjured on its face
The rejection as bitter as brine
War is hatred, the purest of its kind.

What is war to me?
An endless trail of futility.

Ayan Osman (15)
Walthamstow School For Girls, London

Don't Let This Be The Future

We live in a world of darkness
Where no animals can be seen
There's so much brick and concrete
The forests are no longer green

I do not wake to birdsong
But drilling and roadworks instead
The only animals left alive
Are the ones inside my head

As I journey to school
I pick some litter off the ground
Oh, if only people would care some more
The earth is our only playground

When I walk by the skyscrapers and buildings
I notice the remains of an ancient oak
I would've liked to see this beautiful tree
But of course, it's been turned to smoke

In geography we learned about what used to be
Of extinct species and the oceans
Seeing images of dying polar bears
It just brought on so many emotions

I come home rather upset
Thinking of all that could've been done
So many species are dying and dead
There's probably not long left for the sun

Again, I fall asleep to engines
Fumes poison the world every minute
I know we humans haven't long left
When before we thought we'd be infinite

I only wish to be amongst nature
And sing along with the birds
Although we were so different
I felt that we spoke the same words

I wish I could go back in time
And change what has become today
We could have turned things around
Before they had reached halfway

I want to leave you with a thought on planet Earth
It's something you must not forget
This planet belongs to future generations
So do nothing that you'll regret

Lily Bea Deason (15)
Walthamstow School For Girls, London

Black Lives Matter

A bullet away from a hashtag, that's what we are
If the world stays this way, we won't get far
They say racism is dead yet blacks die every day
Slaughtered for their melanin yet they were born that way
Tamir Rice, Alton Stirling, just a few I can name
They say things are changing but it still stays the same

Would you like to explain why they had to die?
To the mothers, wives and families who struggle to get by
Knowing their sons and daughters were taken unlawfully
While society tiptoed around the problem cautiously
Pretending those police did what they had to do
Would you be saying the same thing if it was you?
Mike Brown died saying, 'Hands up, don't shoot.'
Would it be different if he were not wearing a hoodie, but a suit?

Why must the colour of my skin define me?
Open your eyes to what you don't want to see
From the times of slavery to even right now
Why won't you let us be black and be proud?
You try to oppress us but we get stronger every day
We will fight this in each and every way
You can't hide from us, we're everywhere you look
From the music that you listen to, to the way you want to look
Can you believe that the slang you are using

Come from the very people that you are abusing
When will this stop? When will this end?
When can we throw down our weapons and just be friends?

I know words mean nothing to the ones who lost their lives
And it's probably insignificant to the ones they left behind
But we will continue fighting through sunshine or rain
To ensure that those who died did not do so in vain

Renette Bakemhe-Moulton (15)
Walthamstow School For Girls, London

For Pearl

She is watercolour, flowing
But, all at once, acrylic
Staining

At times I have to squint
To see her without
Blinding myself

And I always think
I always believe
Any pain is worth the sight of her

That the sight of her is
Worth never seeing her again
(It always will be)

I want to use my stains
To paint her a picture
Of bronze and sepia and abyss

Because beauty is in the eye of the beholder

And she beholds more beauty
Than I thought could exist

I can see the sun through the window
And how little it compares
To her eyes, lit up like amber
And her smile melting them to flares

And in the early hours
When they are lidded (and she droops)
I can sink into her irises
And see the stars and the moon

For to me
Her eyes are space
Endless, infinite
And I am so small

And so thankful
(Though it may blind me)
To look at her and see this all

And I think to myself
However lost in space
I have her hands to hold me
In my place

So I will paint her a picture
With her as my colour
And my paintbrush in one hand
(And her hand in the other)

And show her how I see her
Psychedelic, dancing
A prism of light

The darkness whispering
A calming, stormy night

She is watercolour, acrylic
She is the entire spectrum
(And although I am blind)
She is all the colour I need

Ronja Blight (14)
Walthamstow School For Girls, London

Fallen...

You wanted her but she washed you out, so why cry?
Why have sleepless nights and feel full of guilt when she didn't bother to shed a single tear?
The urge to meet her one last time is possible yet why do you feel the need?
Why go through all the pain and torment again? She doesn't care so why do you care?
You loved her, she didn't, you wanted her, she didn't she insulted you, you didn't, then why look back to such affliction?
Walk away my love, forget all those useless days she made you sit in agony and cry
Walk away because the day she realises what she had lost, it would be too late
Crying for her is a waste of time because the person who doesn't value your tears is nothing but a complete loser
Scream, weep but never in a million years hurt yourself for her because she isn't worth it
You are, and only you
Forget the one who caused so much distress to you because you know what?
You deserve better, you are one in a million and she couldn't see that
Treat yourself, be happy and live your life to the fullest because the one who injured you will be the one who suffers in the long run
For now, sweetheart, see the beautiful side of life and shine like a shining star...

Shahina Jauny (15)
Walthamstow School For Girls, London

Warriors

See the world around you
What it has become
We are living on a battlefields
Where innocent people are killed
Their wishes unfulfilled

Everyone has to fight
Wrong or right
Tall or short
All sorts
Everyone
Everyone is blamed and hurt just for being themselves
We have to be strong battlers
Be against racism, stereotypes, discrimination and more
We have to be warriors

Look at all the holocaust survivors
Now they were fighters
Fighting to save the lives of innocent Jews
They didn't lose
They were blamed for being evil and vile
Just for having a different lifestyle

Look at all the news
All the false allegations
Why are Muslims called terrorists?
Why are they on the bad list?
Why are they abused?

Why are they accused?
Is this right?

People waking up knowing they have a battle to fight
Fight for their rights
Rights in their life
Fighting with a knife

Torture, slavery
Now that's still going on
People undesirably obeying people acting like a don

These people want to scream
But they can't talk
They want to run
But they can't walk

Struggling, suffering
What's wrong with that?
Everything!
Don't wait
Stop this before it's too late!

Sara Arshad Mehmood (13)
Walthamstow School For Girls, London

Inside Out

Tears stream down her cheek
As she pukes out her meal
Her wrists covered with deep cut scars
Her drawings crying for help
'Too fat, not normal,' she whispers to herself
As they tease and bully her
Alone with the hate said about her weight
Her fingers trembling with fear and her body
Aching with memories
Haunted by the past
Cries herself to sleep each night
Holds back the pain with all her might
Broken-hearted, crushed inside
Too frightened to go out
Too exhausted to smile
She stares at the mirror with disgust
Her eyes lost the sparkle that they once had
Her heart lost the liveliness that it once pumped
'I'm not a doll, I'm a human being.'
'I'm not perfect, no one will ever be, you need to accept me for me.'
One word can destroy and ruin someone so much
Yet no one notices, the dying inside, smiling outside
she hides her sorrow with laughter and joy
Her mates think she's fine but little do they know
She learnt to forgive but couldn't let go

All names and insults that were said
You see sticks and stones *will* break her bones
But words, they *can* hurt, and they haven't stopped since.

Maarya Zahid (14)
Walthamstow School For Girls, London

Memories Fade Away

I've saved a special place for you in my big, red heart
So even though you're in Heaven we're not apart
You taught me how to love and how to stay when things get rough
But at the age of seven, handling all of those emotions was tough

I'm starting to forget all of the small things
I really want to remember, yes I'm trying
It's so hard for me to hold onto the memories
It's like every day another one fades away

You were my biggest fan, you were there through it all
I believe you're looking down on me helping me to cope
But if I'm talking honest I'm not doing too well
Your absence has affected me and everyone can tell

I've savoured every moment that I've spent with you
I can't help but feel like I should have tried harder for you
So are you really in Heaven looking down on me and keeping me safe
Because I wish you were with me, helping me with all the troubles I've faced

I'm starting to forget all of the small things
I really want to remember, yes I'm trying
It's so hard for me to hold onto the memories
It's like every day another one fades away

Aisha Patel (14)
Walthamstow School For Girls, London

Lying Man

He prays to his lord but not to be forgiven
Towards evil intentions his heart has been driven
He has no hesitation on what he believes is right
On defenceless families he forces a fight

He calls himself a Muslim but is drenched in blood
If the tears he'd caused were with him he'd be drowning in a flood
He uses our religion as an escape to get away
But some people are fooled by the lying words he says

He manipulates minds to believe his actions are just
He turns us against each other breaking our trust
But he is the enemy that we need to fight
We need to open our eyes to the true sight

He steals numerous lives without a second glance
We take the blame, just give us a chance
Why should others face the punishment he deserves?
We are outsiders, while he gleefully observes

He stabs his knife in the innocent whilst crying God's name
But why call yourself a Muslim when murder is your game?
Muslims aren't murderers, we don't have blood on our hands
So a terrorist calling himself a Muslim is just a lying man.

Zanib Asim (13)
Walthamstow School For Girls, London

You Can Change The World, You Can Make A Difference

You can change the world, you can make a difference
Make the fighting stop dead,
Make the hate freeze ahead,
Spread peace and love,
with the wings of the white dove.

Banish the war from earth and make it never to come back again,
Drain the evil in a flash,
And make people think about each other's health,
not just money and cash.

Make people do well, not worse
Let's spread happiness through the whole universe!
Make them go from sad to happy,
But don't get too snappy.

Make them see the good of the world, just as we were taught,
Warm up their hearts, from cold to warm,
Let the love go, it spreads like a swarm.
Pop the grumpiness out of everyone's lives
Let's celebrate with some life pies!

Pull out the sorrow that has been sucked in the people's hearts
Don't tell anyone but actually we are all smart!

Smash the weakness into tiny little pieces
Let's make each other some masterpieces.

That's what my grandfather had said when I was a child,
You can change the world, you can make a difference!

Monika Martinonyte (11)
Walthamstow School For Girls, London

One Human

We are one human;
One brain,
And one's flesh and bone,
Who care for nothing but ourselves-
And ourselves alone.
The soils we call land that we do not own,
The weakening souls left to the bone,
Responsible for those deprived of food,
But we on the upper hand aren't screwed-
We on the upper hand have what we desire,
And wealth is all our hearts admire.
Believing we are incapable of seeing behind our back,
As humanity our ignorance really doesn't lack.
We are one human;
One brain,
And one's flesh and bone,
Who care for nothing but ourselves-
And ourselves alone,
Our fake words of sincerity
Pumps disbelief from the heart,
The agony of division that tears us apart,
Praising our leaders who are liars and cheats,
But with them we'll get the higher seats.
we as Mother Nature's mankind
Are capable of more than your narrow mind.
We wouldn't starve our babies,

And we deny what is true,
But if we are one human;
One brain,
And one's flesh and bone,
Then we are responsible for more than just our own.

Aliyah Elizabeth Ahmed (15)
Walthamstow School For Girls, London

Contradiction

You
Are
Everything that I am not.
Everything that I am.
A walking,
Talking,
Living,
Breathing,
Contradiction.

Perfect in height,
Yet too short.
A lovely sight.
Just a bit too...
Fat,
Thin,
Light,
Dark,
Not enough.
Yet too much.
A little bit of a
Perfect mistake.

Welcoming the enemy.
Then pushing him away.
Falling in and out of
Hate.

It's hidden by a mask,
Everything you could be.
A dam
A shield
Created to
Block and
Reflect.

Reflect,
The facts
Not the opinions
The sun
Not the dark side of
The moon.
A shield.
A protective barrier.

'Protective,' you say.
What does it protect?
Who?
Them?
The others?
Probably.
Not you.

Definitely
Not
Me.

Zia Ralston (12)
Walthamstow School For Girls, London

Changes...

How can we eat?
How can we sleep?
How can we do anything knowing
That people's lives are incomplete
People are drowning in the water that we drink
Because we would rather let them sink than to let them in

People these days have less of a worth
Because offenders walk away
Leaving their victims lay hurt
Our weak minds are why there's so much brutality
So we need to take a look again
To find that thing we call reality

We put up a wall saying there
Are no problems in this world that have to be solved
But thinking carefully how have we evolved?
From our old ways, we should be amazed
People are spending days, starving to death
Without a home, trying to raise money all on their own
We have problems, stop praying, get up, solve them
We are the problems to our own damn problems

Destiny Angela Evelyn O'Kane (12)
Walthamstow School For Girls, London

Hope

Bombs! Grenades! Killings!

I close my eyes tight
Tears welling in my eyes
These innocent victims who once laughed and smiled
Now have lost the glow, the spark
Their eyes are full of despair and one question; why me?
I've opened my eyes
What do I see?
Children lying on the ground. Still. Pale. Lifeless

Mothers screaming for them to wake
Nothing. Families trying to escape their home
Which have become foreign
Climbing the boat, their eyes flicker to hope
Hope that their lives can change
Hope that the war they were stuck in the middle of will end
Hope, to return to their external homeland and remake it

I reach out my hand giving them the push they need
Hope, is just a hand away, reach far enough and you will catch it.

Imaan Iqbal (15)
Walthamstow School For Girls, London

My Brother

Almost dog-like, ecstatic when you've gone all silly
Blowing raspberries, sprouting random facts about cars like you've gone crazy
Forever laughing, trying to race you is like going on a wild goose chase
Head bowed down in solemn, when pranks are caught
Fumbling when you nervously try to stumble to class - curious of your new classmates
Staring into space - hoping for class to be over
Eight years have passed since you have been born - it has gone by so fast
Speedy as light, you have grown so much, what a brilliant younger brother you have been
Oh, how much have you grown, my little brother

Ying Hang Zeng (12)
Walthamstow School For Girls, London

The Dustbin Man

When you throw a wrapper,
The wind makes it flutter.
The wrapper might hit the man who is wearing black boots,
Or maybe you might find it under your shoe.
You will take off the wrapper and throw it away,
But no one will be able to throw it in the waste.
When the dustbin man sees you he will say hi,
When he looks at the rubbish he will say why.
The dustbin man starts working really hard,
Picking up the rubbish you have left apart.
He wants to go home,
But because of you he won't.
Instead he picks up your rubbish,
And you don't even appreciate.
You don't know how it feels,
When the dustbin man has to pick up the rubbish that's not his.

Sumbal Arshad (14)
Walthamstow School For Girls, London

Dream

Life is but a dream
What you say
What you do is all a dream
Wake up
See the world...

The bombs you see, the destruction
Shown to the world
But they'll say
It's just a dream

The hope people lose
The dead bodies surrounding them
But life is but a dream

The grief people feel, the food they lack
But they'll say
Go back to bed as
Life is but a dream

Life is just a dream...

Wake up!
All the races
The fights for equality
But
They'll say life is but a dream
Life is but a dream

The truth covered in lies
So...
Wake up
As you are just in a dream

Zara Khan (13)
Walthamstow School For Girls, London

Cultural Contract

It's evolved, has our technology
It's surpassed our humanity
And soon, it too
Will be superior to our identity

Shifting through pages
Of meaningless faces
Through emotion to emotion
Each cleared of all devotion

When an infamous trend
Leads the way
Dictates what we do
What we think, what we say

It's different in my memory
Looks different on the screen
But the camera tells no lies

And the curved glass
And contorted reflections
V the angled flat
Perceptions of the lens

We will always opt
For the manipulated view
Though technology tells no lies

Erin Ridgway (12)
Walthamstow School For Girls, London

Hatred Is My Drive

I don't know and I don't really care
All I feel inside is fear
Struck by lightning, goes up my hair
I say help but they all just stare

Happiness around me
But not inside
I wish I could not see
I just want to hide

They call me names
Boast about their fames
If this is a game
It has turned out lame

But now I've found hope
Pushed the hatred to a side
I held that rope
No more can hide
Motivational moments
I cannot give up
I continue drinking from this cup
The tea of wisdom
Pushes me forward
I continue
fighting
I'm not a coward

Samar Mahmood (15)
Walthamstow School For Girls, London

Before I Die

Before I die
I want to eat all the pie
Mostly I don't want to lie
Before I die
I don't want to see people dying
And hearts lying
Everybody is crying
Before I die
I want to see everyone smile
I don't want to learn textile
But I want everyone to walk a mile
Before I die
I want faces to shine
But not like mine
And to make sure everybody has a spine
Before I die
I would like to say goodbye
Goodbye...
Before I die
I don't want to die
I want to live in peace
I want my life to increase.

Kiran Tanveer (12)
Walthamstow School For Girls, London

Living My Own Life

Being hypnotised by
Everybody's eyes
I'm always being their spy
They're always making me cry
I just wanna live my life

They trample all over my leg
Always throw at me an egg
Where do I have to begin
I just wanna live my life

I'm climbing all the mountains
Drinking from their fountains
Telling me what to do
I say forget you
You don't control me
You don't own me
Making millions of pounds
Fighting millions of round
Cos now I'm living my life

Faiza Mehmood (12)
Walthamstow School For Girls, London

The Forever Life

Death
Heaven
Hell
Life consists of waiting
Hoping
Knowing that every day you're getting closer to death
Wishing that there is
Something
Some place
Somewhere
In this universe
Or the next
That will let us live
Live during death
Forever

Death
Silence
Sleep
Imagine a forever
A forever of nothingness
Wishing to be dead
Somewhere
Some place
In this universe
Or the next
That will let us die

Die during death
Forever

Hannah Billington (12)
Walthamstow School For Girls, London

Revenge

Can't you hear the skull crack?
The darkness is covering the light of your halo; your emaciated body,
Can't you hear the lifeless bodies chanting your name,
Seeking agonising revenge?

Your robe is as crimson as sticky blood,
That oozes out of the warrior's head.
They have come for you, and no one can help you.
The halo on your head has vanished;
It can no longer protect you from your sins
And so,
You must face your punishment alone.

Emine Ulucay (12)
Walthamstow School For Girls, London

Disability

Some may call it racism or even sexism
But no, it's a disability
You may not want to help me
But you do not need to not like me
Just because of my disability
I don't care if you don't like me
Because you think I'm a disability in your life
Your hate will be
The end of you
So go ahead, don't like me
I'll just hide from reality

Hannah Rashid (14)
Walthamstow School For Girls, London

Family

Families are sweet, they are the ones who taught you how to tweet and eat
They're the ones who stood by you and loved you and made you feel special
They're more important than the rest of the world
And they are my world
My family's like a stem, they support me and love me
I love my family and they love me

Amud Ahmed (12)
Walthamstow School For Girls, London

YOUNG WRITERS INFORMATION

We hope you have enjoyed reading this book – and that you will continue to in the coming years.

If you're a young adult who enjoys reading and creative writing, or the parent of an enthusiastic poet or story writer, do visit our website **www.youngwriters.co.uk.** Here you will find free competitions, workshops and games, as well as recommended reads, a poetry glossary and our blog.

If you would like to order further copies of this book, or any of our other titles, then please give us a call or visit **www.youngwriters.co.uk.**

Young Writers
Remus House
Coltsfoot Drive
Peterborough
PE2 9BF
(01733) 890066
info@youngwriters.co.uk